DESERT STORM DIARY

With the
Ten Commandments
of
Muslim Diplomacy

Franklin Hook
Author of *Never Subdued*

Fall River Publishing Hot Springs SD

ISBN-10: 0988579618
EAN-13: 9780988579613
Library of Congress Control Number: 2012953217
CreateSpace, North Charleston, South Carolina

HIS027000 HISTORY / Military / United States
HIS037070 / Modern / 20th Century
HIS027040 HISTORY / Military / Persian Gulf War (1991)

DEDICATION

For my sons, Bill and Paul, who were also overseas
during Desert Storm, my daughter Kari, and all of my
loved ones who were left home to worry.

CONTENTS

FOREWORD

A few days before Christmas in 1990, Colonel Frank Hook noted in his diary: "We have been dangling since August and on alert since Thanksgiving. Lots of war-talk on television." Such were the day-to-day anxieties that bedeviled the author, an Army reservist physician who would command North Dakota's 311th Evacuation Hospital during its deployment to the Middle East during Operation Desert Storm.

The word dangling hardly does justice to the confusion, contradictions, and misinformation that characterized the mustering of the Army's medical resources for service in an arid region some 7,000 miles from the U.S. In large part, the dangling occurred because "certain war planning assumptions did not come true,"[1] and because the Army dithered between full and partial mobilization of its medical units. In addition, there was no nationwide database of reservist medical personnel that could be used to "backfill" under-strength units like Hook's 311th.

Small wonder that after still another snafu, Hook's diary entry was brief and to the point: "g.d. Army!" Nonetheless, when his unit was fully staffed and on the cusp of deployment, Colonel Hook told the men and women who were leaving spouses, families, friends, jobs, and communities for an unknown destination and an uncertain future: "We are all volunteers. Now our nation has called and we must go." With those few words, Hook

---

1   United State Army Reserve in Operation Desert Storm: Reservists of the Army Medical Department. John R. Brinkeroff, Ted Silva, John Seitz. 2400 Army Pentagon, Washington, D.C. Contract #: MDA 903-90-D-0033. p. 9.

captured the volunteer spirit that has bolstered America's armed forces for much of our country's history.

Desert Storm Diary is much more than a diary. It is a narrative of an unfolding war that saw America lead a coalition of more than thirty allied nations to liberate Kuwait from Iraq's occupying forces. It is also a family history, because two of Hook's sons were on active duty at the time. One commanded a B-52 bomber, and the other a platoon of M1A1 Abram tanks.

For the 311th, a large part of the war drama was the challenge of living and working on Arab soil in an Arab culture, and of developing working relationships with their Arab hosts and counterparts. From Hook's experiences in meeting those challenges come his "Ten Commandments of Muslim Diplomacy," wise advice from a thoughtful participant/observer. Another challenge Hook faced was getting and protecting resources that would enable the 311th to do the job it had been sent to do. If anyone believes that rear-area wartime operations are not messy and at times petty, read Desert Storm Diary.

Hook embellishes his work with maps that are useful for visualizing the war theatre, and interviews that give voice to some of the participants. He also includes news articles that provide a civilian perspective of the battalion's activities. Desert Storm Diary is also rich with photos, some of them depicting the machinery of the war, and many more depicting the people involved in Hook's narrative. Happily, Hook has indexed his work.

One wrenching experience Hook describes concerned his son, Bill, the B-52 commander. Hook knew that Bill had been deployed, but knew nothing of his whereabouts. The colonel was in his quarters one evening watching CNN (one of the few reliable news sources available in the Gulf, he says), when he heard that a B-52 had gone down and that three crewmen were missing. Then he heard that one of the missing was from North Dakota. What were the odds that a B-52 crewman from sparsely populated North Dakota was not his son Bill? Hook's heart "skipped a beat" and his eyes "filled with tears." After two fearful days, Hook finally learned that his son had not been aboard the ill-fated B-52.

Perhaps it was Hook's indelible memory of that experience and others like it that moved him to create Desert Storm Diary some two decades after the deployment of the 311th. Such writing can be both clarifying and healing. By then, he notes, "a good number of people" from his battalion have "left this life." For those who remain, however, and for the survivors and friends of those no longer alive, Hook's narrative is a meaningful tribute to the men and women of the 311th. They will especially appreciate his roster of the battalion, a permanent, readily accessible record that will be visited time and again for reminiscence and history. And for those who simply are interested in that brief but powerful event now known as the 1st Gulf War, Hook's Desert Storm Diary is a compelling source of first-hand information.

John Durand Author of *The Boys: 1st North Dakota Volunteers in the Philippines*

PREFACE

This is a story about war. Unlike my first adventure in writing a military history, *Never Subdued,* this story involves my own personal experiences. I had not thought about writing anything about my family's involvement in Operation Desert Storm until Steve Bakken, host of the *What's on Your Mind* radio program on KFYR in Bismarck, North Dakota, asked me if I had anything else upcoming besides my recently released book, *Never Subdued.*

Before I knew it, I blurted out that I had kept a diary during Desert Storm and that my two surviving sons (Bill, a B-52 pilot; and Paul, an M1 A1 Abram's tank platoon commander) had been overseas too—all of us at the same time. Unlike movies such as *Saving Private Ryan* and *The Fighting Sullivans,* the military has no definite policy for excluding family members from serving in the same combat zone, with the exception of a written request for a sole survivor (DoD Directive 1315.5), either bringing one back from the combat zone—or at least trying to—like happened in the movie *Saving Private Ryan,* or preventing the sole survivor from entering combat. On-line encyclopedia Wikipedia states: "The need for the regulations first caught public attention after the five Sullivan brothers were all killed when the USS Juneau, CL-52, a light cruiser, was sunk during World War II, and was enacted as law in 1948. No peacetime restriction was in place until 1964 during the Viet Nam War; in 1971, Congress amended the law to include not only the sole surviving son or daughter but also any son or daughter who had a combat-related death in the family. Since then, each branch of the military has made its own policies with regard to separating immediate family members".[2]

More recently, Texas brothers Lance Corporals Cody and Bobby Henrichsen celebrated the holidays at home before deploying to Afghanistan. The Henrichsens are among five sets of brothers deployed with the 1st Battalion, 23rd Marine Regiment based in Houston[3].

There is nothing unusual about three members of our family serving overseas in wartime. As it turned out, only two of us were in the combat zone, and only one of us, Bill, saw any significant action. Yours truly saw only one missile in the air, after spending several hours sitting on my flak jacket during a medevac mission, that might have been an enemy Scud (or a chasing defensive Patriot), treated one non-traumatic patient, and spent the rest of my time performing the administrative duties of running a four-hundred-bed hospital. Nevertheless, some of my colleagues had interesting experiences, which I have related here, and my diary documents the history of the conflict, including my angst about my son Bill when a North Dakota boy was reported missing after a B-52 bombing run.

---

2   *Wikipedia*
3   -http://blog.chron.com/armedsources/2011/01/5-sets-of-brothers-to-deploy-to-afghanistan-together

ACKNOWLEDGEMENTS

No one can write a story that is ready for publication without lots of help. Therefore, my thanks go out to Col. John L. Jacobsen, the 311th Pharmacist and my Deputy Commander for his unit history *A Story of the 311th Evacuation Hospital during Operation Desert Shield-Desert Storm: 2 Aug 90-17 Mar 91*. Also, in composing and writing the official after action report of the 311th Evacuation Hospital, Command Sgt. Major Jerome L. Braxmeyer, as well as LTC Jim Miller, my executive officer and a previous 311th Commander, gave me lots of advice and help.

In addition to conversations with my two sons, Colonel Bill Hook, Medical Corps, USAF, who at the time was B-52 Aircraft Commander Captain Hook, and my son Paul, who was at the time 1st Lt. Paul Hook, Tank Platoon Commander, I also gained unusual insights into the workings of a B-52 crew through a personal interview with Air Force Senior Navigator and Air Operations Commander Colonel Mike Tichenor. After Desert Storm Tichenor, who was then a Captain, became Bill's navigator. They are also brothers-in-law—they married sisters.

Thanks to LTC Bruce T. Gilmore, who was the officer in charge of the Enemy Prisoners of War (EPW) Medical team we sent to Kuwait to process the thousands of prisoners who were suddenly overwhelming Army resources. Dr. Gilmore wrote the after action report on that assignment. Also, thanks to Col. Terry Brosseau, past Executive Officer of the 311th, Viet Nam combat veteran, Bismarck's MedCenter One Administrator at the time, and my cousin, whose persuasiveness got me into the Army

Reserve but without whose knowledge and experience that he passed along might have suffered a less fortunate fate for the 311th.

Not to be excluded from my appreciation are all of the members of my command staff, including LTC Helen Johnson, who proofread for factual errors, and the amazingly hard-working people of the 311th, who made our mission of caring for all casualties—both civilian and military—in the combat zone such an overwhelming success. Also, we had unexpected and critical support from our sister services of the Air Force, the Navy, the Marines, and the Diplomatic Corps as well as Host Nation organizations. We returned those favors on many occasions.

The most helpful with advice and critique was John Durand, noted author from Elkhorn, Wisconsin. John wrote the Foreword to the manuscript. He is the author of *The Boys: 1st North Dakota Volunteers in the Philippines*, a well-received history of the regiment."

Having served on active duty in both the Navy—including a year at sea—and the Army, and with one of my sons being a career Air Force officer, my only conflict now involves deciding whom to root for at the inter-service games (My friends know whom I favor!).

Franklin Hook, autumn 2012.

INTRODUCTION

My father once told me that since the time I was born there has been no peace in the world. Somebody somewhere has constantly been waging war. His words are as true today in the twenty-first century as they were in the 1940s and 1950s. Back in the late 1980s and early 1990s, I, like most people, was busy living my life.

It was an exciting time to be a radiologist. New technologies had been made available by significant progress in developing new patient imaging modalities like CT Scanning, ultrasound, MRI, and Gamma cameras. These technologies had resulted from our space programs and the National Aeronautical and Space Agency (NASA), and all of them made information available to visual image interpreters such as myself to a degree that was overwhelming. I still remember everyone referring to the tiny white specs on MRI images of the brain in some sequences as UBOs (Unknown Bright Objects) because no one knew what they were. Now, of course, after years of experience with interpreting, most of those spots have fallen into known categories—both normal and not so normal.

The first clue that my professionally exciting life would soon be interrupted came with the escalation of worrisome events in the Middle East during the summer of 1990, which were caused by an aggressive dictator in Iraq called Saddam Hussein. This ruthless jerk had used chemical weapons on his neighbors in Kurdistan, who disagreed with his assertions that they were citizens of Iraq.

"Iraqi Kurdistan first gained autonomous status in a 1970 agreement with the Iraqi government and its status was

ix

re-confirmed as an autonomous entity within the federal Iraqi republic in 2005."[4] The Kurdish territory also extended into Turkey and Syria, and there was a Kurdish Provence in Iran. Not all of them were autonomous.

In July of 1990, Hussein was amassing troops on Iraq's border with Kuwait.

The following diary entries are footnotes to a greater picture that I, along with many others, observed and participated in from the fall of 1990 until the Ides of March in 1991. They tell a story of anxiety, emotional trauma, and war, the latter of which combat veterans often describe as weeks of boredom interspersed with moments of stark terror.

However, there is more to it. Ours was largely a support mission, and although we had moments of fright, we were mostly just doing our normal jobs of taking care of patients. While the pre-deployment training, which occurred in the deep snow in January with temperatures well below zero, was probably the most physical discomfort we experienced, the emotional experience of being separated from loved ones is something that most of us will never forget, especially given the anxiety of not knowing what we would experience nor for how long.

So come along, dear reader. We won't scare you, but I think that you will come away with admiration for our young service men and women. I hope that by noting the sacrifices—sometimes of lives—you will feel secure in our nation's abilities. There are none like them in the world.

---

4   *Wikipedia* Kurdistan

DESERT
STORM
DIARY

PROLOGUE

Setting the Stage:

*O*n January 28, 1991, eleven days after American fighter-bombers launched the first air attacks against Iraqi positions that had been holding Kuwait in its grip for the previous five months, Newsweek Magazine stated that one of the turning points on a deadly path to war had been in Late July 1990, when a few mid-level intelligence officers predicted the invasion of Kuwait in spite of their superiors disagreeing.[5]

There was no doubt in the minds of officers in the Army's Reserve 311th Evacuation Hospital that *Newsweek* had understated what was thought and experienced by reservists like us during those months when Desert Shield was turning into Desert Storm. We were under constant stress as we anticipated the alert that would be followed by a mobilization order called *Roaring Bull.*

The tension continued to build as summer turned to fall. Lives were going to be interrupted; we could feel it coming.

---

5   *Newsweek* Special Issue 12/28/91 p-56

The aforementioned mid-level intelligence officers were vindicated on August 2nd when Saddam Hussein's troops crossed the border under the pretense that Kuwait had been stealing Iraqi oil by slant drilling. Saddam also accused Kuwait's Emir Jabir Al Sabah of depressing world oil prices and suppressing OPEC production[6] and also accused him of expanding the Kuwaiti border forty-five miles into Iraqi territory while Iraq was busy fighting Iran in that recent conflict.[Ibid]

Newsweek also suggested that sources in the U.S. Intelligence Agencies had assumed that Hussein was trying to bully Emir Al Sabah into accepting a policy more to his liking, and concluded that the danger of anything more than rhetoric was unlikely. *Newsweek*'s writers included the Defense Intelligence Agency, the State Department and the CIA in their vilification.[7]

I guess it's easy to be a Monday morning quarterback if you are a journalist who depends on briefings from so-called insiders, but those of us who had actual information—or at least thought we did—were worried. My son Chris, who was an industrial engineer working in Japan at the time, later scoffed at my references to Army Intelligence as "an oxymoron." He may have been right, but then again, his Grandfather Boothe, a Stanford graduate and WWII Navy veteran, often referred to Chris's University of California alma mater as "The People's Republic of Berkeley," suggesting, of course, that liberal-leaning Berkeley graduates were ill-informed.

As it turned out, once we were overseas, the only direct intelligence provided to our outfit came primarily via CNN and an occa-

---

6   Ibid. p-58
7   Ibid. p-57

sional worrisome briefing from US Embassy personnel in Abu Dhabi. Other sources of insightful or strategic information included the Air Operation Centers at Bateen and Al Dhafra Air Force Bases, which were just a few miles from our Host Nation Hospital, Al Mafraq, about twenty kilometers outside of Abu Dhabi in the United Arab Emirates.

Mafraq Hospital was staffed and paid for by the UAE Royal Family, and it served all UAE civilians and Coalition Forces during the war. The civilian doctors, who took care of civilians, were contract physicians from neighboring countries such as Iraq, as well as the United Kingdom and Europe. The 311th took care of all military personnel and coalition member civilians and responded to a number of Al Mafraq physicians' requests for consultations.

In my first entry in a leather-bound diary, as I anticipated the war that was to follow, I mistakenly recorded on the wrong line Saddam's border crossing, which had turned into an obvious invasion, and I recorded it in two words: "Kuwait Invasion." Because I did not have the diary until November, I mistakenly recorded the event as having occurred on the August 7th line, while the actual crossing had occurred on August 2nd. Later in an undated portion of the diary I recorded another short note: "Bush orders Reserve call-up." Thus began the cycle of emotional stress in which the 311th received intermittent alerts. The 311th must have been placed on or off the Essential Force List (EFL), at least a half dozen times.

The Chief Medical Officer, Col. Scheiweiss, of the 426th Medical Group in the 96th Army Reserve Command (ARCOM) in Salt Lake City had warned me weeks in advance that I might be asked to resume command of the 311th. Scheiweiss informed me that it was Army policy for a physician to be in charge during wartime. Colonel Jacobsen, the 311th historian, described it like this:

"From the day of the invasion, reserve forces were targeted by FORSCOM (Forces Command) for duty in support of Desert Shield. The 311th Evacuation Hospital in North Dakota was placed on alert several times from the invasion date until 21 Dec '90. The hospital at that time was under the command of LTC James R. Miller, MS. (Medical Service Corps). During this time-frame of August to December 1990, the unit had specialized instructors from Readiness Group Denver brief the unit members on mobilization procedures, as well as the history of Saddam Hussein and his use of chemical agents against the Kurds in Iraq."[8]

There were also extensive administrative lectures and procedures on such things as the preparation of wills, powers of attorney, soldier's rights, and so forth. Mobilization packets had to include copies of marriage licenses, divorce papers, next of kin contacts, birth certificates, and countless other data, all of which kept the 218th JAG (Judge Advocate General's Corps) Detachment, who shared our facility, very busy. They were the Army's legal experts, lawyers, and judges.

Upon my return from a medical meeting in Chicago in late November 1990, the situation had changed again, but despite all of the on-off placements on the EFL, the 311th was soon on a fast track to the Middle East, and we landed at Bateen Air Force Base (AFB) in the United Arab Emirates on January 17, 1991, the very night that the first missiles fired from Apache helicopters hit targeted enemy radar stations in western Iraq at 0238.[9]

---

8 Jacobsen. *A Story of the 311th* (p. 6)
9 Lowrey, Richards. *The Gulf War Chronicles* (p. 3). Universe Star, Lincoln, NE 2003.

CHAPTER 1

AUGUST 1, 1990–DECEMBER 28, 1990. Prelude to War: Alert and Mobilization

In wartime, truth is so precious that she should always be attended by a bodyguard of lies. —**Winston Churchill**

*A*t a meeting on August 1, 1990 in Irkutsk, Siberia, Soviet Union, U.S. Secretary of State James Baker diplomatically suggested to Soviet Foreign Minister Eduard Shevardnadze that the Soviets should try to restrain Hussein.[10] Baker was referring to Saddam's forces being amassed at the Kuwaiti border. It was one of those rare moments in history when President George H. W. Bush and Soviet President Gorbachev agreed to appear united against a common threat, as recorded by Newsweek's Margaret Garrard Warner.[11] Actually, Baker was enroute to Mongolia—supposedly on a hunting trip— when the meeting took place. He had to delay his travel plans the

---

10 *Newsweek* Special Issue 12/28/91
11 Ibid. p. 54

next day when Saddam's troops crossed the Kuwaiti border, and he eventually cut his trip short to go to Moscow to develop a joint US-Soviet statement with Shevardnadze.

Despite suggesting that there had been a massive intelligence failure in their January 28 Special Issue, *Newsweek* praised the speed and size of the Coalition Force that Bush had put together.[12] *Newsweek*'s Peter Turnley noted that Bush had organized the Coalition, which included Arab League States, industrial democracies, and some members of the United Nations, and then assembled his own invasion forces—the highest concentration of troops since D-Day in 1944.

In the August of 1990 section I made my first entries in the leather-bound diary that my wife Linda had given me. In two other entries in August, I acknowledged the birthdays of my oldest son, Bill, who had turned twenty-nine on the fourteenth, and Paul, my youngest boy, who had turned twenty-four on the fifteenth. Bill was still at K.I. Sawyer Air Force Base in the Upper Peninsula of Michigan, and I had no word on his overseas deployment. As the commander of a B-52 crew, his work was classified. I worried because I knew that with air-to air fueling they were capable of doing a long-range mission overseas and then returning to the States.

Paul was already stationed overseas, commanding an Abrams M1-A1 tank and crew in Germany near the Czechoslovakia border. I was unable to reach him, but I had sent him a card and check a week earlier. In my diary entry, I indicated that the boys'

---

12 Ibid

mother, Margo Boothe Turkington, "thinks he is on alert but has not deployed".

In my next diary entry on September 10, 1990, I also acknowledged the birthday of my middle son, Chris, who had just turned twenty-seven. "He is working as an industrial engineer in Japan after getting his Master's in Business at Berkeley. Notes people in Japan do not appear to be concerned by the events in the Middle East."

In an undated and unidentified newspaper clipping in my possession, Japanese spokesmen later indicated that: "Criticism of Tokyo's less-than overwhelming contribution to the anti-Iraq effort could aggravate relations between the world's two top economic powers."[13]

Although I made no further diary entries for the rest of September and October of 1990, dialogue and rhetoric about the threat of war were alive and well on CNN and other news outlets. In addition, during this timeframe the violence between Jews and Palestinian Arabs escalated, the United Nations carried out their usual peacekeeping talks, and George H.W. Bush's Coalition Forces were building strength in the region:

- 17 September: *Time Magazine* reports thousands of Kuwaiti refugees on the roads between Iraq and Jordon.[14]
- The month of September: The UN Security Council passes no less than five resolutions concerning Iraq and Kuwait, in addition to many other resolutions concerning

---

13 Scrapbook by 311th Auxiliary
14 http://www.time.com/time/magazine/article/0,9171,971155,00.html

Israeli- occupied territories, Lebanon, Israel itself, Syria and Iran. There is a lot of talk but no significant action.

- 8 October: Seventeen Palestinians are shot and killed, and over one hundred are wounded by Israeli police at the Al Aksa Mosque on Jerusalem's Temple Mount, a site sacred to Jews and Muslims.[15]

- By the end of October there were an estimated five hundred thousand Coalition troops in the Gulf. At its peak, the Coalition had mounted over three quarters of a million people. "In 1990–91, the United States deployed a total of 527,000 personnel, over 110 naval vessels, 2,000 tanks, 1,800 fixed-wing aircraft, and 1,700 helicopters".[16]

Britain, one of the largest contributors of the Allies, deployed 43,000 troops, 176 tanks, eighty-four combat aircraft, and a naval task force. Saudi Arabia, an even larger contributor, sent fifty thousand troops, 280 tanks, and 245 aircraft. France, Egypt, and Syria also contributed serious forces and assets.

"Other allied nations, including Canada, Italy, Oman, Qatar, and the United Arab Emirates deployed a significant portion of their small forces."[17] Of the fifty countries that contributed, thirty-eight of them deployed air, sea or ground forces.[18]

I made my diary entries for November 16 and 17 while we were doing a normal drill weekend called a Multiple Unit Training Assembly, or MUTA. The services love acronyms and they

---

15   http://www.thepeoplehistory.com/october8th.html
16   http://www.answers.com/topic/gulf--war
17   ibid
18   Scott   Williams,   Maj.   USMC,   http://www.dtic.mil/cgi-bin/ GetTRDoc?AD=ADA405987

are worse than the medical profession in their use of acronyms. During the MUTA, multiple units trained at the same facility, which in this case was the Lewis and Clark Army Reserve Center in Bismarck, North Dakota. In this particular instance, the Center accommodated the 311th Evacuation Hospital, the 945th Engineering Company, the 218th JAG Detachment, and likely a couple of others during the same weekend.

After the regular drill on Saturday the 16th, MSGT Dale Rummel, the facility chief of the 311th, asked me to stay so that he could tell me something. I knew right away that the news would not be good, since the media was escalating its talk of war. Sure enough, the World Wide Command and Control System (which we called WOMAX and others called WIMAX for short), indicated that we were back on the Essential Force List (EFL).

WOMAX is a computerized system that gathers, organizes and communicates classified vital information. The World Wide Military Command and Control Systems keep track of all USA military units in the world, their location and what is planned for them. One can only imagine the secrecy levels this system encompasses. The expert on this behemoth is a Professor of Sociology who teaches at the University of Texas, Brownsville. His name is David E. Pearson, and if interested I refer the reader to the internet source below.[19] His thesis can be viewed at the footnote internet source and was published by Air University Press, Maxwell Air Force Base, Alabama. Pearson is a graduate of Am-

---

19   http://aupress.au.af.mil/digital/pdf/book/b_0076_pearson_command_
     control_system.pdf

herst University, earned his PhD at Yale and completed a fellow-ship at Ohio State.

MSGT Dale Rummel was an experienced senior NCO who was skeptical at times of the Army bureaucracy. I was also skeptical but played more of a "let's wait-and-see" attitude. As it turned out according to my observations, the bureaucracy usually forged ahead without always fully exploring the consequences and worried about correcting mistakes later. It was often the on-site commanders who solved problems and I actually believe the solutions were mostly provided by those who were on location at the scene, and if it was a military facility usually with the help of senior NCOs like Rummel, Terry Milas, Jerry Braxmeyer or Jeff Campbell.

The real problems seemed to arise when those further up the chain-of-command ignored the assessments or pleas from those beneath them. Witness the autumn 2012 fiasco in Benghazi, Libyia where our Ambassador and three security guards were murdered. Also note John Durand's comment in the Foreword of this book or the differences expressed by Generals Schwarzkopf and Franks later in the text.

In my diary, I wrote: "Dale thinks it may be another mistake. Still no word on DepMeds." DepMeds refers to Deployed Medical Equipment or Medical Equipment placed in a Depot overseas. Thus a MASH or EVAC Hospital can fall in on their stored equipment and go to work. "Word is we're still far out on the list. Dale thinks it may change again"[20]

---

20 Hook Diary Nov. 17, 1990

The next day, Sunday November 17, Dale and I went out to Bismarck's National Guard Headquarters at Fraine Barracks and got a look at their WOMAX. We were still on the Essential Force List with a potential mobilization date in early December, which was about three weeks away, and they had us leaving for MOB (mobilization) Station shortly thereafter in order to be overseas by January 9, 1991.

I was getting nervous and starting to re-evaluate our situation. The 311th Tactical Standard Operating Procedure states that our mission is "To provide hospitalization to all classes of patients in the combat zone." More specifically the Army Medical Department states that an "Evacuation Hospital provides General, Thoracic and Orthopedic Surgery services as well as specifying Neurosurgery, and medical care in Ophthalmology, Internal Medicine and Gynecology. It also prepares patients for further evacuation as necessary."

Prior to the August 2nd invasion and into October 1990, the 311th was on the Essential Force List either because it was our turn on a rotating basis or—more likely—because we had high marks from a recent ARTEP (Army Training Evaluation Program). The only things that kept us on a lower level of the Essential Force List were the lack of surgeons and 91 C's. 91 Charlie is the Army MOS (Military Occupation Specialty) designation for practical nurse or combat medic. I was concerned about figuring out where to get the doctors and medics we need to complete our mission if we are mobilized.

My diary entry for Monday, November 19, the day after the MUTA drill, indicated that Dale Rummel had called me at home after the drill and "said that 6th Army had made the same mistake about our equipment and we were to be off the EFL today, the 19th."[21]

In the same entry, I wrote: "Fat Chance! Back on the List this afternoon and the word is it's for real. We'll have to wait and see. I made a phone call via Dale to the 426th Medical Group in Salt Lake City before we went to Fraine Barracks yesterday. Col Scheiweiss confirms that they want me to take command again."

In my diary entry for the next day, Tuesday, November 20, I noted that I had left my Chicago hotel number with Dale (MSGT Rummel) because Linda and I were traveling to attend the annual gathering of the RSNA. The Radiological Society of North America's annual meeting in Chicago is the largest meeting of radiologists and associated technologists in the world. It has fantastic displays of the latest in X-Ray, CT, MRI, ultrasound, and nuclear imaging and therapy equipment, as well as educational exhibits, lectures, and interactive teaching programs. The RSNA did such a great job housing and herding between twenty and thirty thousand participants all over Chicago and the McCormick Center that the organization elected to make Chicago the permanent location—after trying a number of other cities—of the annual gathering. There was no doubt in my mind that things were escalating for us and it was not just rhetoric on TV.

The following day, Wednesday, November 21, I noted in my diary that I had transferred Larry Tessmer, our warrant officer physician's assistant, to a slot reserved for a family doctor because I knew his capabilities and I did not want to lose him to some unknown or inexperienced practitioner. In order to do this, I had

21   Ibid. Nov. 19, 1990

to re-assign one of the Minot section's physicians from a family doctor (he was a pediatrician) to an Ear Nose & Throat (ENT) position. I also noted that we would have two more registered nurses than we had been allotted if all the authorized transfer fill-ins, which are called NAADS (New Army Authorized Documents System), showed up at our mobilization station in Fort McCoy near Sparta, Wisconsin.

In my next entry, I noted that I had spent Thanksgiving Dinner with my wife's sister and her family, the McAllisters, in Steele,

Warrant Officer CW3 Larry Tessmer, a talented physician's assistant

North Dakota. I then had a second helping with my sister's family, the Karlgaards, in Bismarck. I noted that my mother, Ann Franklin Hook, looked healthy but her hearing was bad. The holiday was a nice but brief break from the events that were about to overwhelm us.

I don't remember specific conversations from that Thanksgiving Day, but the atmosphere was tense with worse-case scenarios at both locations. Linda's brother, George Allen Rohrich, was in the active Air Force Reserve, and was a candidate for coming into harm's way too. I wondered how many families were affected. It had to be hundreds of thousands.

One Friday, November 23, I wrote in my diary: "Helen Johnson (LTC Helen D. Johnson, a senior RN) stopped by to discuss a medical problem. Helen was an essential member of my staff who was in charge of both Operations (S3) and Intelligence (S2), and I did not want to lose her to some minor problem. I told her to get herself in shape and arranged an appointment with a specialist to do so (She did). I left my Chicago number with General Bagley's secretary at 96th ARCOM." The 96th Army Reserve Command in Salt Lake City controlled Army Reserve Units in seven states.

On Saturday, Linda and I flew to Chicago. We arrived at the Holiday Inn to find a message waiting for me from MSGT Dale Rummel. ARCOM had forwarded an official Alert for the 311th and they wanted me back for a change of command. In retrospect, I should have probably resisted, but Dale had already made flight reservations for my return on Monday. Linda was not happy. We had dinner that night at the Italian Village.

The next day I returned our complimentary tickets from the Phillips Corporation for a Broadway show, cancelled a dinner meeting with Siemen's representative John Eichenberger, and cancelled Linda's site-seeing tours. I did manage to attend a lecture on disc diseases at McCormick Center. A friend of mine, Dakota Medical Systems Representative Warren Wormager, saved the evening by taking us to dinner at Biggs on Dearborne Street

On the flight home, I filled in a lot of entries from memory and loose-leaf notes in the new diary that Linda had bought for me.

On arrival, I found out that we had been moved down on the list and although we were still on alert, our mobilization date was not as imminent. I could have stayed in Chicago. My diary entry was short: "g.d. Army!" I guess I was thinking about the Jeep driver from the movie *M.A.S.H.*

In the November 26, 1990 issue of *Newsweek*, Oilman T. Boone Pickens flatly stated that we were involved with Desert Shield to secure the oil supply. While he did not advocate war, he wanted the embargo to work. He noted that although the U.S. was perceived as the most powerful nation on earth, we couldn't even get our deficit under control, and predicted—rather prophetically—that it would grow to four hundred billion dollars in two years (I wonder what he thinks of the multi-trillion dollar debt and deficits today).

In my diary entries for the November 27 and 28, I noted that while we were still low on the Essential Force List, we were bouncing around on mobilization dates on the WOMAX. In addition, Forces Command wanted our doctors to be in San Antonio so that those who had not gone through basic training could do so, and the press called wanting to know if we were on alert. I referred them to a Public Affairs Officer in Salt Lake City.

Wednesday, November 28: *Bismarck Tribune* this a.m. quoted ARCOM (the public affairs officer) as saying, 'the 311th has no imminent possibility of mobilization.' It would be nice if ARCOM knew what the hell was going on! We get more up-to-date data from National Guard WOMAX. Miller's wife is threatening to write a letter to the editor." Jim Miller, the current Commanding Officer of the 311th, was going to become my Executive Officer after the change of command. One problem that ARCOM's misinformation caused was that some of our soldiers believed the media despite the official alert notice, and they left town without leaving phone numbers with our administrative staff.

A month later, after 96th Army Reserve Command's misinformation—which *The Tribune* repeated—the ARCOM officer in question showed up to assist with releasing information to the public as we mobilized. I changed my initial negative impression when I saw him wearing a number of campaign ribbons. When I questioned him about his knowledge of our mission, our personnel, our location (three sections in three different cities), and our numbers, however, he drew a total blank. I let him know in no uncertain terms that I was unhappy with his actions and that as a result of them we had to chase down a number of our members who had wandered all over the country, as well as dealing with the problem of jammed phones lines at the center when we were scrambling to get additional personnel and equipment. I may have actually embarrassed Jim Miller, who overheard me chewing the Major's rear end. I had learned that correcting errors through education worked better than scolding. So, rather than continue the verbal abuse, I just left the major with a number of things to read, including information about the organization and equipment of an EVAC Hospital, the Table of Organization and Equipment (or TOE), and the basic mission of the unit. I doubt that he completed the tasks before he returned to Salt Lake City. Until we left, the information he publically announced was tainted with errors. I never saw him again.

The after action report confirmed the problems created by a less-than-knowledgeable public affairs officer, the most serious of which was the loss of troop whereabouts accountability. Fortunately we caught up with the locations of our wondering personnel and recovered them in time for mobilization. The recovery process was not without effort and put more stress on our already overloaded phone lines.

Near the end of November, the UN finally gave Saddam a deadline of January 15 to get out of Kuwait. In retrospect, we should have guessed we would be in country and ready to work by the deadline. As it turned out, General Schwarzkopf wanted all of his medical resources to be in place before the shooting started. Thus, it was a remarkable coincidence that our chartered 747 later landed at Bateen AFB, United Arab Emirates at approximately 0230 local time on January 17—just before the first official shots were fired at 0238.[22]

"On 29 November 1990, the Security Council adopted Resolution 678, authorizing the USA-led coalition to use 'all necessary means' against Iraq to liberate Kuwait if it did not withdraw by 15 January 1991. Instead, the Iraqis reinforced their positions along the southern Kuwaiti border, and by 8 January they had an estimated thirty-six to thirty-eight divisions, each nominally 15,000 strong but actually considerably less. The coalition eventually had about 700,000 troops in the theater, with the main ground contributions coming from the USA and important contingents from the UK, France, Egypt, Syria, and Saudi Arabia, under the operational command of

---

22 http://www.answers.com/topic/gulf-war. ibid

US Gen Schwarzkopf. The maintenance of the coalition, in which Arab states were arrayed with infidels against another Arab state, was pivotal. It was therefore imperative to ensure that Israel—a target for Iraqi missile attacks—should stay out of the war. The Iraqis were known to have the means to deliver their chemical and biological weapons (CBW) with their al-Hussein missiles, which had a range of 373 miles (600 km), double that of the original Soviet Scud missiles on which they were based."[23]

By December 1, 1990, we had acquired information that our "in-country assignment will be Oman Host Nation Support. Word is, we will fall in on an existing facility and we are not to bring existing equipment except OCIE.[24] [We] will deploy with two other Evacs and some Medical Detachments. WOMAX shows major Meds at Dhahran and Riyadh. It looks like we are establishing 1200 to 1500 bed facilities on top of Host Nation's. Our next higher HQ is 202 Med Group out of Jacksonville, Florida. Got call from them today. They are moving to MOB station. We will send advance party to Oman along with one other EVAC, a total of twelve people."[25]

The next day I got a call from Linda's brother, George Allen Rohrich. I knew he had access to classified information in his position in the Air Force Reserve. He stated that he couldn't talk

---

23 ibid
24 I have no clue what OCIE means for sure; it's not an official acronym. My best guess is that it means Overseas Command Issued Equipment. Damn acronyms!
25 *Hook Diary.* December 1, 1990.

on the phone due to being monitored. Then he asked me if my anniversary was on Dec. 28. He knew damn well that it was in August. I asked if he meant the date of marriage. He answered, "No, the honeymoon." This was a secret way of him telling me the overseas deployment date. Backing up that would mean anticipating a Roaring Bull Message about December 7, which was Pearl Harbor Day." I was two weeks off.[26]

The next three weeks were a blur, but I noted the highlights in my diary:

- December 3: Mandan North Dakota's Military Police Unit got their Roaring Bull Message today. ARCOM received the message on Sunday but withheld it until Monday, even though they could have informed all members as they were drilling.
- December 4: The 328th General Hospital from Salt Lake City popped up on the Alert List and got their Roaring Bull Message all at once. They are going to Germany.
- An internal operations order indicated that our new higher headquarters, the 202nd Medical Group, was going to control all USA medical units in the host country of Oman. The location of the 311th is designated to be a suburb of Muscat on the coast of the Gulf of Oman.

---

26 Ibid. December 2, 1990

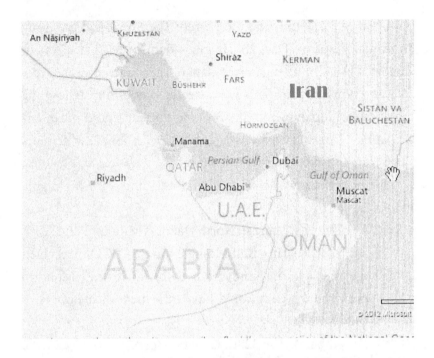

Map: (above) Note position of proposed assignment near Muscat, Oman vs. the eventual one near Abu Dhabi, United Arab Emirates. Both locations are less than 8 minutes by air (for a fighter jet) from Iran. Riyadh is about 400 miles from Abu Dhabi. Map courtesy of National Geographic modified by author.

- December 7: Our higher headquarters told us that they were just awaiting a signed agreement from the host nation, Oman, before they would send the Roaring Bull Message.
- Drill weekend on December 7–8. We got caught up in the Preparation for Overseas Movement, which is expressed with yet another acronym: POM. We had a Christmas party for dependents on Sunday; there was a big turnout and people were very emotional.

- Rumors and facts fill our senses and become as one. It is difficult to separate facts from rumors. The bottom line on Oman was that the Host Nation Agreement never materialized. We would not know when or where we were going for a while.

December 19–20: "My high level of emotional stress continues. We have been dangling since August and on alert since Thanksgiving. Presidential Order #39 has started to deploy units close to us on the Essential Force List. Three inches of snow this eve. Cold! Bush and Saddam are arguing about when to meet up with Secretary Baker. There is a lot of talk about war on the television."

I noted in my diary that General Bagley had called my house but I was not home. I knew he had been raiding other units because he had promised to get us filled to one hundred per cent of required personnel. I knew we were still short on surgeons, especially orthopedic surgeons. On Friday December 21, Bagley called me back and said he had thirty two more people including some surgeons but we were still short of orthopods. I know he has raided every asset he has in his seven state area, but he said that 6th Army, based in California could have more, perhaps inactive reserves.

The General thinks we will get the Roaring Bull message between Christmas and New Year and said that we could do the change of command any time. I told MSGT Rummel to time it to the Roaring Bull message as planned.

December 21:"Guess what? The Roaring Bull message came in to the National Guard WOMAX at about 0630 this a.m. before

Bagley called me back. He didn't know it either! I got it at 0915 at work at MedCenter One. We had to warn ARCOM that the message was in the system and that got them looking. I took the rest of the day off to work at the Reserve Center."

I am now officially on active duty, and I informed my radiology colleagues: Drs. Pablo Ramos, Al Hill, Bill Cane, John Doerner, and Brad Meyer. Hill or Doerner will likely fill in as Department Chairman until I get back. I asked Al Hill, a fellow pilot, to fly the Cherokee once in a while to keep it current, and he agreed. Since I was taking a significant drop in pay, Al also agreed to pay the plane's expenses so that he could use it. I had previously checked him out in the Cherokee 235, and I felt comfortable with his skills. We are both instrument-rated.

Within the next two days, ARCOM and Bagley filled us to the point where we were ninety-five percent Military Occupation Specialty (MOS) qualified. Since we had plenty of registered nurses but were short of combat medics, ARCOM moved some of the RNs into the 91 Charlie slots—a process they called cross leveling. I noted the process in my diary and called it "a good move!" I also noted that we were still short a neurosurgeon, an ENT, and at least one orthopod. The cross filling was also noted in the after action report.

On Christmas day I took on-call duty for my civilian radiology colleagues because I was scheduled for it and a quick change in our call schedule would have caused inconvenience and disruptions. I also would have felt guilty, even though I could have gotten out of it. It wasn't too bad anyway and I was still available to make command decisions for the 311th.

The day after Christmas MedCenter One, the primary hospital that our x-ray department served, held its annual Christmas party. In the diary I noted: "Tom Rowekamp [Major John Thomas Rowekamp] and William Wood [Captain William C. Wood] have their hands full in logistics. Helen called and said that the media was at the MedCenter Christmas party. They love to play on emotions and I had a lump in my throat when I made some remarks. Of course it showed when it was broadcast on TV. One of my officers broke down completely."[27] KFYR TV won an award for that one.

Photo above of LTC Helen Johnson and MedCenter One's Joyce Baldwin. Bismarck Tribune December 27, 1990

27　Ibid. December 26, 1990

Tribune article of 12/27/1990. Reprinted with permission.

After Weeks of Waiting Hospital Unit Gets Call

Dressed in Army Camouflage, Dr. Frank Hook joined his coworkers at MedCenter One for a goodbye celebration Wednesday. "The desert sands are white and grand deep in the heart of Persia" yodeled someone during a party of cake, hugs, handshakes and kisses.

"Get outa here", the doctor said, laughing.

Until this week Hook was the chairman of Q and R Clinic's radiology department. He is now the commander of the Army Reserve 311th Evacuation Hospital which is mobilizing to leave for Fort McCoy Wis., on Sunday.

Headquartered in Bismarck members of the 311th have been watching events of the Persian Gulf since Iraq invaded Kuwait in early August.

The status of the 311th seems to have mirrored the flow of hopes for peace and the ever increasing risks of war.

"In August we went on the essential force list," Hook said. "We went off the list in September and on again in October. The day after Thanksgiving we went on alert and we were activated last Friday.

Gulf: an emotional time. Continued from page 1A.

"It's been an emotional roller coaster", he said, "Our families have been up- and-down."

If war breaks out units like the 311th will be very busy. "Our mission is to take care of all classes of patients in the battle zone," Hook told the Tribune. Formerly called a M.A.S.H. (sic)[1] unit (Mobile Army Surgical Hospital), the 311th is a 400 bed hospital with 19 doctors and related staff members. In battle they attend to any and all that need it. "That means civilian and military from psychiatric to trauma (battlefield wounds) cases," Hook said.

The greatest number of 311th members from Bismarck-Mandan with full time medical careers work at Medcenter one and Q and R Clinic. Those employees were treated to a going

---

[1] The Tribune erred. An Army Evac Hospital is more than twice as large as a M.A.S.H. and has always been called an Evac.

away party Wednesday and it was mostly upbeat.

There were occasional sniffles, a few tears and many fearful questioning looks as friends and coworkers tried to comprehend the meaning of the reservists' imminent departure.

"We're sure going to miss you. Come back soon and safe," dietary technician Hulda Schulz said to nurse Helen Johnson.

From now until the end of her assignment, Johnson will be addressed as Lt. Col. Helen Johnson. At MedCenter One she was a nursing manager. In the Army she will be responsible for unit training of nurses.

Hers is largely an administrative role, but Johnson said she is capable of rolling up her sleeves if casualties start pouring in. She is one of few 311th members with combat nursing experiences, having served in a US Army Hospital in Japan during the Viet Nam War.

Johnson said that besides family she'll miss church and work at the hospital.

She is chairman of the board of deacons at Trinity Lutheran Church in Bismarck, a post she handed over to an assistant. "She'll also be missed in the church choir," said Joyce Baldwin the hospital switchboard operator. "We sang in the choir together. We go back a ways, 15 years."

In the medical community the impact of those leaving will be minimal. Johnson said contingency plans were laid months ago in case of a call-up. Other hospital employees will step in to pick up the slack where vacancies were created.

St. Alexius Medical Center will have one employee called to active duty as will Mid Dakota Clinic.

Hook said his job has been eased by help from the North Dakota National Guard. "Generals (Alexander) McDonald, (Robert) Shulte and LTC Gary Doll have really helped with transportation", he said. "This has been the largest mobilization in the state so far and it's quite a job".

Until Sunday's departure 311th members living within 50 miles of Bismarck will be sleeping in their own beds and commuting to the Lewis and Clark Army Reserve Center. The others arriving from Minot and Fargo and other in-state and out-of-state communities will be housed at a local motel. Fort McCoy is a jumping off point for reservists and National Guard soldiers who have been called to active duty. The 311th, Hook said, will be there anywhere from 3 to 14 days.

Although the unit's likely destination is Saudi Arabia, Hook said there are several possible scenarios. If in Saudi Arabia the unit could be sent to an existing Saudi hospital or an existing temporary facility.

The unit could be sent to a host nation in the surrounding region such as the United Arab Emirates or Qatar, dispatched to a base in Germany or Italy, or be retained stateside at an Army Hospital.

The unit could even be split up with members sent to other mobile Army units around the globe.

Thursday, December 27: "MOB Day! Troops have been pouring in all day. I have Terry Milas[28,29] and his crew meeting planes and providing buses to motels and the Reserve Center. I gave a commander's briefing and made remarks to locals. Channel 12 picked it up."

From Col Jacobsen's history: "At 0730 hours on 27 December, the first formation and roll call was done.-The ARCOM brought in a POM (Preparation for Overseas Movement) team to again check the MOB packets and to prepare payroll records.-Showdown Inspections were being conducted continuously during this period.

On Friday, December 28, I gave the commander's briefing to a crowd of about three-hundred newly transferred soldiers and dependents:

"Season's greetings and welcome to active duty and Operation Desert Shield. For those of you who don't know me, my name is Colonel Franklin Hook and I am the Commander of the 311th Evacuation Hospital.

"I'm sure you have many questions, such as 'Who is this guy?' 'Where are we going?' 'For how long?' 'Why are we here?' and so forth. In the next few minutes I'll try to answer as many of these questions as I can.

"Why are we here? You and I have heard all of the arguments. Congressional and public debate has filled the airways for months. Although I am not a politician—but rather a phy-

---

28 ibid
29 Terry Milas was a senior NCO, formerly a unit 1st Sergeant for the 311th. He did not deploy with us due to a transfer to the Engineers. If memory serves me right he was in Iraq or Afghanistan some 10 years later.

sician—I, like you, have personal opinions. In the long run they don't matter, but perhaps I can at least try to put it in perspective for you. It's not about oil—exactly. And it's not about the defense of Kuwait—exactly. And it's not even about Saddam Hussein's blatant aggressiveness—exactly. Certainly the role of the United States, the greatest democracy that has ever existed, and its responsibilities to the United Nations and the free world have to be considered. We, as citizen soldiers, have to help meet that responsibility.

"It's about all of the above. Oil figures into the equation not because of the defense of cheap prices at the pump or because of adequate supplies, but rather as currency, the flow of wealth. Oil as currency is not only the lifeblood of the free world, but if misdirected it becomes the sustaining power of a malignancy so aggressive that if allowed to grow and metastasize, which it has already done, it would nurture the tumor and eventually kill the host.

"You and I know what I am talking about. We are medical professionals and we have fought cancer all of our professional lives. We know that when dealing with a malignancy we treat it early, as early as we can if we are to have any hope of survival for our patients. The method of treatment for cancer is usually open to debate. In my institution, a cancer committee, called a tumor board, carries out the debate. When all possibilities of treatment are considered, whether they are radiation, surgical excision, chemotherapy or a combination have been discussed, the attending physician evaluates all options and makes a decision. He or she bases this decision on the best information available and on what he or she believes is best for the patient. A committee cannot treat cancer.

"An analogy in the Persian Gulf situation is that Congress and the public constitute the cancer committee and our Commander-in Chief, President [H. W.] Bush is the attending physician. He has the awesome responsibility of choosing the proper treatment. Saddam Hussein and his cohorts are a malignancy on the face of humanity. The cancer must be dealt with. If surgical excision—that is, war—is selected as the treatment, we know that some good cells will likely be destroyed in getting rid of the malignancy. We will try to keep the number of good cells that are lost to a minimum.

"'The Preservation of Life' is the motto of the 311th Evacuation Hospital. That is why we are here, ladies and gentlemen, fellow professionals: 'The Preservation of Life!' We are the instruments of that motto, the bottom line. We are all volunteers. Now our nation has called and we must go.

"Those of you who have been assigned to us from other units, such as the 396th Station Hospital in Helena, MT, the 406th Combat Support Hospital from Denver, CO, the 447th Medical Detachment from Grand Forks, ND, and others are joining a first-rate outfit. When I was last Commander, we scored nearly perfect in our most recent ARTEP, the Army's Training Evaluation Program. My immediate predecessors, Col. Obert and LTC Miller, have maintained this high level of training.

I then introduced my administrative staff to the crowd (See appendix A) and then continued with the briefing.

"Who is this Guy? I'm a local product—a graduate of Bismarck High School. My father and mother were local schoolteachers.

I graduated from Stanford University, California and Jefferson Medical College of Philadelphia, and I served three years in the Navy as a physician. I practiced Family Medicine for three-and-one-half years, and then I returned for specialty training in radiology. I am certified in both radiology and nuclear medicine, and I have been in practice for nearly thirty years. I consider myself a pretty fair diagnostic and interventional radiologist.

I am married and have four children. Two boys are currently on active duty. One is a B-52 Commander and the other a Platoon Tank Commander who is now overseas. So, like many of you I have loved ones who may come into harm's way."

I then introduced my wife, Linda, and my oldest boy, Captain Bill Hook and his wife Debbie. They were aware of our imminent deployment and they came to see us off. The briefing continued.

"Where are we going? Your guess is probably as good as mine, but let me give you some possible scenarios."

I then gave them a whole list of possibilities, including Saudi Arabia, Turkey, Oman, and UAE in the Middle East; Germany and Italy in Europe; and CONUS (The continental USA). All of the possible assignments included fixed facilities like hospitals in the host nations, and since we were a MUST (Medical Unit Self-contained Transportable), I also included a scenario with our inflatable structures, which were operating rooms, lab, x-ray, and hospital beds. Another possibility was that we could have been split up, with our assets and personnel going elsewhere.

Then I addressed the last major question, "For how long?" The short answer: "For 180 days unless extended." Two months later, the Army did indeed extend our stay to one year. Fortunately, it was not necessary and we were discharged from active duty in March 1991.

CHAPTER 2

DECEMBER 29, 1990–DECEMBER 31, 1990.

American Potluck: The New Guys

It ain't the individual, nor the Army as a whole, but the everlasting team-work of every bloomin' soul. —**J. Mason Know**[30]

They came from every background imaginable, and as I started to interview the new doctors, nurses and support personnel, I felt blessed. Back during the Viet Nam era they were called FNG's (friggin' new guys), but there was nothing new about their qualifications and experience. I will use the term FNG again, but to me it will always mean Faultless New Guys. The 96th Army Reserve Command had done well with their raiding and cross leveling.

Dr. Gil Roman (pronounced Row-M'awn) was not a doctor of medicine but a doctor of education. Gil was a bird Colonel (O6) in the Medical Service Corps who had served as the execu-

---

30 http://inkstainswithroni.blogspot.com/2009/08/inspirational-quotes-poems-sayings-for.html

tive officer of the 5502nd U.S. Army Hospital in Aurora, Colorado. He had extensive experience, in logistics and in personnel, commanding a holding company. A Latino who was multilingual, Col. Roman became so valuable to the Army of the United Arab Emirates that they decorated him for his services.

Above: Col. Gil Roman being decorated by a UAE officer. Also being decorated is 1st Sergeant Jeff Campbell the 311th's 1st SGT, and the middle figure in the picture. Campbell was a Viet Nam vet from the 1st Air Cav., and one of our finest. Photo credit: Col. John Jacobsen.

Before we go further, let me explain the Army's system for assigning an alpha-numeric code for a soldier's job or occupation. It's called an MOS which is another acronym meaning Military Occupation Specialty. It has no logical reasons for the alpha-numeric codes that are given other than some bureaucrat started handing them out.

Most physicians wound up with MOS numbers in the 60s or 61s followed by an alphabet letter. Mine, as a radiologist is an "R" so I am a 61R, but Dr. Wade, who is a Urologist, is a 60K, which probably means that the bureaucrats were referring to kidneys. I can only begin to imagine why an Orthopedic Surgeon would be a 61M (perhaps "muscles") or an Ophthalmologist would be a 60S (perhaps "sight"). At any rate, we used the phonetic alphabet when referring to the designation so that a practical nurse or combat medic would be a 91 Charlie and a medical-surgical nurse would be a 66 Hotel. You can see all of the MOS designations in the alphabetical roster in Appendix C, and the Phonetic Alphabet is listed in Appendix F.

Phil Spiegel was another O6 Colonel—an orthopedic surgeon from Tampa, Florida. Phil was a graduate of Northwestern University. He experienced active duty like I did in the nineteen sixties, possessed a Master's degree and an MD, and had extensive trauma surgical experience (Phil was not on the final alpha roster and he was transferred. He may have been the Orthopod that was not deployable).

Capt. Dave Brooks, a 67 Bravo (Field Medical Assistant) was a graduate of Cal Poly and a trained NBC (Nuclear, Biological, and Chemical Warfare) officer and teacher. Dave was from Missoula, Montana.

John Wade, a 60 Kilo (Urologist) was from Billings, Montana and he had twenty-eight years of surgical experience. LTC (O5) Wade was a tall, imposing man. A graduate of Wayne State University who trained at John Hopkins in Urology, he turned out to be a real asset and I was glad to have him. John also had extensive experience in transplants and belly and bowel cases, and he was a certified Flight Surgeon.

Don L. Bishop, another 61 Mike (Orthopod) and bird Colonel (O6), was a graduate of McGill who trained in Orthopedics at Temple in Philadelphia. Don was from Helena, Montana and he specialized in foot and hand surgery. He had twenty years of experience in trauma surgery. John spent some time on active duty in Thailand during the Viet Nam War, and he could handle an arthroscope.

Gary Peterson was a medical ophthalmologist (60 Sierra) from Great Falls, Montana, and he was another O6. He was a graduate of Tulane Medical School who interned at Sacred Heart in Spokane and took his residency at Mayo in Rochester MN. Gary was an award-winning photographer with an interest in astronomy. He hadn't done any eye surgery since 1982, but our mission did not require eye surgery. He was another O6 Colonel. You could tell from the number of colonels that our doctors had a lot of experience.

Larry Cook, a Chief Warrant Officer, was going to be the unit's chief ordnance officer. When I learned it was going to be a criminal violation to bring along any weapon that was not listed in our armory, I immediately donated my .38 Magnum to the armory and CWO Cook made it legal. The weapon was decommissioned on our return to the states. When I asked the chief if he had any special qualifications he answered, "Beucoup" and he did. Among other things, he had experience with automotive body repair and maintenance, and he was an armorer, an award-winning marksman, a Humvee[31] expert, and a heavy equipment instructor. Larry is a special man and I appreciated his skills.

Tad Gilmore, (61J) was a certified general surgeon with two years of active duty in the Air Force. Tad was a graduate of the

---

31   HMV or HumVee is an acronym for High Mobility Vehicle

University of South Carolina's Medical School, and he had trained in surgery at Denver's St. Joseph's Hospital. An O5, LTC Gilmore had been a Presbyterian missionary in Kenya and Swaziland before settling in Greeley, Colorado. A surgeon with twenty years of experience, Dr. Gilmore felt comfortable in all areas of his specialty. He ended up leading the Enemy POW medical processing team into Kuwait as the war was winding down.

These were just a few of the new ones, and I was running out of time to talk with all of them. I would get to know a lot more of them during the next three months. Their collective skills and talents were extraordinary to say the least, and I haven't even started on the personnel that I know.

Saturday, December 29: "I picked up General Bagley at the airport at 2300 last night. Both of us are here at the Reserve Center preparing for the Advanced Party departure to Fort McCoy tomorrow. I am planning to send Col. Roman along with the Advanced Party in order to beef up the logistics section. His resume is amazing. I had lunch with my daughter Kari, and Bill, Debbie, and Linda. It is probably the last time I will see Kari for a while."

Sunday, December 30: "No sleep. By the time I got packed it was 1:00 A.M. I stared at the ceiling for two hours and then got dressed and went to the center to see the Advanced Party off. Some tears. I spent the rest of the day putting out logistics fires. I found out that we needed more trucks to get everything in, but there were no trucks anywhere. Finally, I called a golfing buddy, local businessman Steve Herman, who owns Ryder Truck Rentals. He came through. It's bitterly cold. Steve had to spend a couple of hours thawing out trucks to get them started. He asked no questions about how he was going to get paid. We need more patriots like him. I slept for a couple of hours in the afternoon."

Above SSG Tim Rasset a member of the 311th advanced party looks adoringly at his tearful spouse, prior to deploying on Dec. 30, 1990.[32]

Monday, December 31. New Years' Eve Day: "Last eve was family night. I said my goodbyes to Mom, my sister Pat, Dick, and my nephew Joey. Kari was out of town. I got very little sleep. I was up at 0400 to the Center. Lots of tears. Chamber of Commerce and MedCenter One provided donuts and coffee. One of my chaplains broke down completely during a prayer. He recovered nicely by saying, 'Chaplains cry too.' I gave a TV interview and then headed off to McCoy."

In an article in *The Bismarck Tribune* on December 31, 1990, Associated Press writer Phyllis Mensing made note of the patriotic sendoff that the 311th Evac hospital got from the Regional

---

32 Tim Rasset died in 1999 at age 51. His widow, Dianne still resides in Mandan, ND.

Army Commander Major General Donald Bagley, Salt Lake City, North Dakota Governor, George Sinner, and Bismarck Mayor, Bill Sorenson.

The short send-off ceremony at Bismarck's Lewis and Clark Army Reserve Center on Airport Road was held on Sunday, December 30, and the unit left early on New Year's Eve day for Fort McCoy near Sparta, Wisconsin. Mensing also noted that Governor Sinner had quoted former president John F. Kennedy and his brother Robert on the nobleness of serving one's country. Mensing quoted Bagley, the two-star General from Salt Lake City who was in charge of the seven-state 96th Army Reserve Command (ARCOM), as saying that the 311th was heading to Fort McCoy to be trained in chemical and biological warfare before being sent overseas. She also quoted Bagley as saying to the troops "You have to have faith in your country, soldiers. You have to believe that what you are doing is the right thing."

The Navy boarding procedures are a tradition. In the Navy, senior officers are the last ones to board a ship, vehicle, or plane, and they are understandably the last ones off, with the exception of reaching a destination. The Army has no such tradition. I'm afraid I ignored my Navy training and fled the TV cameras with a quick kiss for Linda and jumped aboard the first bus before the tears could catch up with me. Some twenty-plus years later, I have a lump in

By LONNIE BERTSCH of the Tribune

"You have to have faith in your country, soldiers," Maj. Gen. Donald Bagley told the group.

my throat with the flood of emotions and the memory of that moment. We were off to war and no one knew if we were coming back.

I imagine that the service men and women of today's forces go through the same experience, only now the recalls are worse. The odds of getting hurt or killed in the combat zones in Afghanistan, Iraq, or elsewhere are much higher than they were in Gulf War I. Ours was a milk run by comparison, but we didn't know that at the time. The emotional toll before the fighting started was high—less for us, but more for our families, who would have to go through the hardships of separation. Things got a little easier as the miles piled up on the way to McCoy. It was New Years' Eve after all. We arrived around 8:30 P.M. and celebrated the New Year in our new—to us, at least—barracks in old Fort McCoy.

CHAPTER 3

JANUARY 1, 1991–JANUARY 17 1991. Fort McCoy:
Training in Snow for the Desert

General Barnicke: Where have you been, soldier? John Winger: Training, sir. Barnicke: What kind of training? Winger: Army training, sir. —**The Movie *Stripes***

*I*t was Tuesday, the first of January 1991 and our opening formation outside of our several barracks buildings in Fort McCoy was a sight to behold. The temperature was hovering around twenty degrees below zero and I stood before some four hundred soldiers in field jackets and parkas whose collective breath raised a visible fog over the ranks, joining the smoke from the chimneys, which were heated by coal-fired furnaces and water heaters. The steam from these devices filled the radiators that hissed and rattled throughout the ancient wooden barracks.

Since I had no public address system, I knew that the slight breeze in the atmosphere over the shivering ranks of soldiers would surely carry my words away before they could be heard.

There was no good solution. I wanted to let them know how important the upcoming training was going to be and to assure them that regardless of what we might have to face, I would do my best to bring them all home intact.

I don't remember what I said. I do remember having to cup my gloved hands around my mouth and shouting while turning my head side-to-side to send the words to the far ends of the huge formation. To this day, I don't know if anyone heard a thing.

My diary indicates that the opening formation and the roll call took over half an hour. Jim Miller had given me an intensive briefing the night before on the hot and heavy training schedule we had to complete. After the roll call, I wrote the following in my diary: "Spent the day at POM (Preparation for Overseas Movement). We got new ID Cards, which were green for active duty. Everyone received three shots, one in each shoulder and one in the butt, for meningococcal meningitis, flu, and gamma globulin for hepatitis and other viruses. Our Readiness Improvement Manager (RIM) is Major Satherwhite. We then received our afternoon briefs."

The next couple of days included more of Major Satherwhite's briefs, a program called Train the Trainer, which prepared us for the intense NBC (Nuclear, Biological, and Chemical) warfare training that we were about to endure. We then were issued more cold-weather gear for the troops.

Although we were just a couple of weeks away from overseas deployment, the reality of NBC (Nuclear, Biological and Chemical) warfare was suddenly thrust upon us, and the intense training lasted twelve to fourteen hours a day. We knew Saddam had used chemical agents on the Kurds. We had also been familiarized with MOPP (Mission Oriented Protective Posture) Gear from previous training, but not to the degree and intensity of these sessions, which lasted the better part of two days. By the time it was over, most of us could don and clear the mask (for MOPP 0) and sound an alarm in nine seconds and get into those suits and masks and be buttoned up in less than eight minutes (for MOPP 3 or 4).[33] I wondered how quickly we would perform under pressure and in extremely high temperatures.

The reality of how close Saddam came to using his arsenal of weapons is illustrated by an interview I ran across some years later in 1996. Patrick Clawson and Daniel Pipes interviewed Rolf Ekeus in *Middle East Quarterly*[34]. I wouldn't have given it much credence except for Ekeus's credentials. At the time of the interview, Ekeus was the head of the United Nations Special Commission tasked with dismantling Hussein's arsenal of long-range missiles and weapons of mass destruction, a position he had held since the commission's inception in 1991. He was my age. Born in 1935 in Sweden, he had joined the Swedish Foreign Service in 1962. Ambassador Ekeus served in various diplomatic positions throughout the world until he began to represent Sweden at the UN in capacities that mostly involved disarmament. From 1989–1993 he was Sweden's leader to the conference on Security and Cooperation in Europe. The interview, published in March 1996, took place January 4 of that year.

---

33 MOPP gear included carrying a syringe filled with atropine, an antidote to nerve gas. We were supposed to inject ourselves right through the chemical suits if symptoms developed. The higher the MOPP (threat) number the more gear you had to wear.

34 Patrick Clawson and Daniel Pipes. *Middle East Quarterly*. March 1996.

Speaking about the state of the arsenal in January 1991, when we were at McCoy and before the shooting had started, Ekeus had this to say:

"In January 1991, Iraq was just months away from having one nuclear weapon. Because Iraq only would have had that one device, it had to have a reliable means of delivery. It could not rely on dropping the bomb from an airplane, not being certain that a plane would get through."[35]

Ekeus went on to explain that Iraq would have had to rely on a missile delivery of the weapon, but although they were making progress, the problems of payload, missile range, and power were yet to be overcome. Hussein did, however, have twenty-five long-range missile warheads that could deliver biological and chemical weapons, Ekeus said, and Iraq was known to have used chemical weapons against Iran.

When asked why Iraq did not use these weapons during the Kuwait war, Ekeus answered that U.S. Secretary of State James Baker had warned Tariq Aziz, Iraq's deputy Prime Minister, that if Iraq used WMDs the U.S. would respond with a nuclear weapon. This exchange apparently happened in Geneva a week before the war started.[36]

In my diary for the next couple of days, I lamented my lack of sleep and my worries that the powers that be would take some of the RNs that we had slotted in the 91 Charlie (combat medics) positions. Then all of a sudden we knew where we were going.

---

35 *Middle East Quarterly.* March 1996
36 Ibid

Thursday, January 3: "I am up at 0500 with four hours of sleep. I have orders to meet with Fort McCoy's post Commander at 1645. I thought it was a courtesy visit, but it turned out to be an initial evaluation. We are in good shape with our replacements. I hope they don't take our commissioned RNs who are in the 91 Charlie slots, but they say they will if need be.

Friday, January 4: "EOC (Electronic Operations Center) called and said that there was a classified message from FORSCOM (Forces Command). I went over to see it with Miller and Roman. We are supposed to send a six-person party to meet with the Minister of Health of the UAE next Wednesday. Miller swears it's bogus. I bet him a dollar it wasn't. He lost. The advanced party will leave on Sunday."

We then had long discussions about who should go on the advanced party. I was anxious to go myself so that I could be sure about what we were getting into, but my executive officer and other advisors convinced me to stay with the unit. Since I was responsible for them, I had to agree.

"I finally decided on Miller, Roman, Jane Geidt (Col. Jane Geidt, Chief Nurse, whose husband LTC Doug Geidt was one of our nurse anesthetists), Moyer (Col. Gerry Moyer, a senior General Surgeon) and Captains David Brooks and William Wood, both 67 Bravos, Field Medical Assistants. The message had specified an ER Doc, an RN, Logistics, and contract agents for local services."[37]

After seeing the advanced party off at 0400 on Sunday I headed for the .45 caliber firing range, where it was so bitterly

---

37 Hook Diary Jan. 5, 1991.

cold that I couldn't feel my fingers. I couldn't even shoot well enough to qualify until it warmed up around 10:00 a.m. when I finally did well enough to qualify as a sharpshooter.

"I am very tired with these eighteen-hour days. Linda was mad because Sharon Miller got more phone calls than she did. I wish she could see my fatigue."[38]

On Monday, January 7, I found out we would be in a fixed facility about twenty kilometers southeast of Abu Dhabi. It was a hospital with modern equipment and open-heart surgery capabilities. They wanted us to work in civilian clothes, which created a whole new logistics problem for us. Where was I going to get the money to buy civvies and the extra duffel bags to carry them?

The host nation hospital apparently had 163 doctors on staff and it was only about thirty percent occupied. They also had a different system for utilizing lab and x-ray technologists, nurses, and other support staff than we did. It would be an education.

We continued to have adjustments in personnel. On Wednesday, January 9, we got more physicians, but we lost two of our own original physicians the next day. Doctors Carlos Torres and Nacasio (Nick) Trinidad were declared as excess personnel in their specialties, and they were transferred. Major Torres, a field surgeon (62 Bravo), went to a clearing company, and Captain Trinidad, a psychiatrist (60 Whiskey), went to the 207th Evac Hospital. We were still shy one neurosurgeon, one orthopod, and one ENT.

We did pick up another medical-surgical nurse (66 Hotel), which told me they would leave our RNs in the 91 Charlie (combat medic) slots.

---

38 Ibid. Jan. 6, 1991.

On January 9 I noted that I had completed HMV (High Mobility Vehicle) training and that the Humvee was quite a vehicle.

From Jacobsen: "PFC Nora Beehler was classified 'excess' in her MOS, and was needed by another unit. Maj. Holly Dieken, a dietician, was also reassigned."[39] I didn't worry about that transfer. We had LTC Corliss Trom, who was a great dietician from my own institution, MedCenter One.

January 10, 1991: "The United Nations Secretary General Javier Perez de Cuellar will leave shortly for Baghdad in a final diplomatic effort to avoid going to war against Iraq. Saddam Hussein is under UN orders to pull his soldiers out of Kuwait within five days."[40]

This was my last diary entry before going overseas. The diary entry below was written on January 19, but it reflects our last week at McCoy:

January 19, 1991: "The last week at McCoy was a blur. Doing a land navigation course in the woods, I promptly got lost with my group. We tramped through snow that was knee-deep to waist-deep. I came down with the Fort McCoy crud, which is a severe tracheitis/bronchitis. Everyone has it. When I briefed the troops before we left, everyone was coughing and hacking. It sounded like we were in a tuberculosis ward. Jet lag didn't help. We left for Volk Field around 1915 on the 15th. We stopped at Kennedy to refuel and I gave Linda a quick call. We left Kennedy for Brussels around midnight. After the crew change, the aircraft was refueled and we arrived at Bateen AFB outside Abu Dhabi

---

39   Jacobsen. *A Story of the 311*[th] (p.11)
40   http://www.thepeoplehistory.com/january10,html

between 0200 and 0300 local time on the 17th. Miller was on the ball with getting buses for the troops. Our 747 could not land at Al Dhafra because it was hot with tactical missions.

The supply flight also left McCoy on January 15, but it was later than the main body. Quoting SGT Brian Fahlstrom[41] on January 15, Jacobsen said, "We left McCoy at 2200 hours for Volk Field by military van. The aircraft had been previously loaded but it did not depart until 0730. We headed for McGuire AFB in New Jersey and arrived at 1030 hours. At 1730 the plane was ready for departure to Germany. At 1900 hours all flights leaving the U.S. were grounded because of the start of Desert Storm."

The 311th had a lot of talented people. One of them, Captain Brian F. Gilchrist was a feisty young surgeon who reminded me of myself at that age, early thirties. In later years he became a renowned pediatric surgeon. He was also a syndicated newspaper columnist. On the following pages is one of his columns that was published in *The Boston Globe, The Memphis Advocate, The Springfield Union,* and likely others between the 20th and 22nd of February 1991. Although the column was not published until just before the ground war started, Brian wrote it shortly after we arrived. It has been reprinted with permission from Dr. Gilchrist.

---

41   Jacobsen. *A Story of the 311*[th] (p. 18)

Above left is Brian Gilchrist, a pediatric surgeon in later years. Above right is SP4 Annie Tavary, a 91 Fox, a psychiatric specialist who is one of the 311th soldiers with her M-16 who is described in Captain Gilchrist's column on the next page.

A surgeon's view from Saudi Arabia

We flew onto the Arabian Peninsula as bombs were dropping on Baghdad. We were 500 strong out of a place called Sparta, Wisconsin, and we were designated the "311ᵗʰ Evacuation Hospital." The soldiers, yesterday's mail men, waitresses, mechanics and nurses strapped their M-16s to their uncalloused shoulders.

It was all so incongruous to watch so many mere girls grasp their gas masks where yesterday they held their babies. They are truly America's heroes of America's rich soil and richer ideals.

These soldiers come from Bismarck, North Dakota, and Billings, Montana and the Springfields of Missouri and Massachusetts, and they are so young, fresh and muscular in both dreams and body.

The girls have eyes the color of Wisconsin's blue glacier lakes, the boys the angular features of their Nordic ancestors. Our richness as a nation comes from the richness of these youth, and it is a richness unsurpassed now or ever.

The boys talk with the bravado of the uninitiated, of the non-combatant and it is apparent they have never seen a badly injured patient or a burned or bombed baby. One wonders how they will respond and perform. The test won't be long in coming. Soon they will witness the brutality of war and modern weaponry

They will care for injuries unseen in civilian life: mortar, chemicals and automatic rifle injuries, foul flesh and singed souls. Again you wonder how will they react. I can tell you. They will perform heroically, magnificently, with the grace and temerity of lion, the lion that our American youth epitomizes.

They have left their homes, their jobs and their babies to care for the combat troops, to give sustenance in an hour of great danger for the world. Some have put aside their political opinions to come here because somebody's son or daughter will need their caring hands.

They saw 400,000 Americans in danger, collected as an island in the midst of a hostile world, and they have arisen to meet the challenge of need. They have each of them, proved American greatness and capacity for sacrifice for those ideals usually only talked about, enunciated by Madison, Jefferson and Lincoln.

And watching them-each of us scared, of that make no mistake-I come to a conclusion about those who do not support the troops. I say shame on you. These troops are out there believing that our way of life and our children's way of life and Kuwait's liberty are at stake.

Shame on you who taste this good life, this free and limitless life and never realize that liberty's cost is real, composed of sweat, of fear, blood, flesh and sometimes life itself.

It now must be clear that we cannot live in a free pluralistic society, enjoying our CD players and driving cars from every point on the globe without realizing that there must be a cost for such freedom. Our freedom is real, so real that the world looks to us for a new life every day, as the disenfranchised continue to stream to our shores as they always have.

And now over the past decade we have lost a freedom, the freedom from fear as the Husseins and other terrorists

bomb our planes, assassinate our Marines in Lebanon and make us fear to attend sporting events. And so we are faced with a grave undertaking, but an honorable cause-to stop an evil that if left unchecked will eventually strangle us.

The choice is not easy but it is correct. We will succeed because of those who have come, those who have joined the fight for our very existence. We are right to be here. Just ask the troops, or better yet, just look at them.

CHAPTER 4

JANUARY 17, 1991–JANUARY 31 1991. Desert Storm: The Shooting War and the Battle of Khafji

Life is a lot like toilet paper. You're either on a roll...or you're taking shit from some asshole. —Unknown

I t was still January 16 in the States when President George H. W. Bush announced the start of the Coalition air campaign. Desert Shield suddenly became Desert Storm. At Bateen AFB we loaded aboard the buses that Executive Officer LTC Jim Miller and the advanced party had organized for us. An AP writer published General Schwarzkopf's message to all Coalition troops in Stars and Stripes on January 17, 1991, stating that it was unknown if the General spoke directly to any particular group.[42] Other publications also repeated the nine-sentence message that Schwarzkopf released from his bunkered headquarters in Riyadh. The message was preceded by a chaplain's prayer and followed by

---

42 AP article *Stars and Stripes*, Thursday, January 17, 1991 (p. 24)

Lee Greenwood's recording of God Bless the USA, which according to some had become somewhat of an anthem for Desert Storm. The General did speak directly to around a hundred occupants of his basement war room at Central Command Headquarters.

Schwarzkopf's message:

> "Soldiers, sailors, airmen and marines of United States central Command: This morning at 0300 hours we launched Operation Desert Storm, an offensive campaign that will enforce United Nations' resolutions that Iraq must cease its rape of its weaker neighbor and withdraw its forces from Kuwait. The president, the Congress, the American people, and indeed the world, stand in support of your actions. You are a member of the most powerful force our country, in coalition with our allies, has ever assembled in a single theater to face such an aggressor. You have trained hard for this battle and you are ready. During my visits with you I have seen in your eyes a fire of determination to get this job done quickly so that we may all return to the shores of our great nation. My confidence in you is total. Our cause is just! Now you must be the thunder and lightning of Desert Storm. May God be with you, your loved ones at home, and our country."

Col. Jacobsen: "We landed in Abu Dhabi, UAE around 0200 local time at Bateen Air Force base. It was January 17, 1991. Armed guards in trucks that resembled the old three-quarters-of-a-ton trucks immediately surrounded the aircraft. We were directed toward waiting buses and loaded onto them still wearing our field jackets with liners and our long johns. Those with weapons, but no bullets, carried them.[43]

Jacobsen also noted that the temperature was around seventy degrees Fahrenheit, and we all broke into sweats in a short period of time. We reached our destination, Mafraq Hospital, around 0430.

"We got off the buses and did a formation in the parking lot of the hospital behind the brick walls and fencing. While we were in formation, a truck backfired with a loud bang and everyone hit the deck wondering 'who's shooting at us?'"[44] The reaction certainly reflected the state of our nerves. We sheepishly dusted ourselves off and reformed our formation.

After formation all of the troops retreated to their assigned hospital rooms which had been vacated to accommodate the Americans. They then gathered in the hospital dining room while still in their BDU's (battle dress uniforms) to enjoy a light snack that the hospital had provided. The excitement increased when I informed them that the shooting war had started. I asked them to return to their rooms and get into civilian clothes because the UAE was nervous about possible terrorist attacks on uniformed members of the Coalition. No one wanted to sleep, but it was too early in the morning to meet with any of the hospital's administrators or staff. Things settled down after assuring some nervous doctors and nurses that we were several hundred miles from the action and that even if there were early casualties we would not be seeing them for a while. Most of us gathered around radios or hospital televisions to get any news we could—and there was a lot.

---

43 Jacobsen "A Story of the 311th" (p. 16-17)
44 Ibid-p-17.

Meanwhile, the Supply Flight was still having their problems: "On the morning of 17 January, the flight was again readied for departure to Germany, leaving at 0800 EST for Ramstein AFB in Germany.[45] On 18 January, 0425 UAE time, we left Ramstein for Al Dhafra AFB UAE. The flight was ordered to return to Ramstein after about an hour and a half because of a Scud attack in the Gulf, which was launched against Israel. Arriving back at Ramstein at 0730, we spent the rest of the day in the passenger terminal with no beds, waiting for clearance to depart again. At 2145, the flight finally departed Ramstein for the UAE. On 19 January at 0100 hours we were ordered to land at Terrajon AFB in Spain due to a defective fire extinguisher on one of the four jet engines."[46]

January 18, the day after our arrival, CNN was the best TV source available to us—and everyone else—and Kuwait's U.S. Ambassador Sheik Saud Nasir Al Sabah, who was also quoted by the Associated Press,[47] indicated that Allied forces appeared to be concentrating their heavy bombing on military targets along the Kuwaiti border with South Eastern Iraq.

The hospital administration and our logistics people decided that the 311th should move into tents until more permanent housing could be arranged. This would free up about 250 beds for potential patients. Though it was still winter, it was relatively mild during the day, but the hot season was looming on the

---

45 Ramstein is in Landstuhl, Germany a little over one hundred miles from Frankfurt; interestingly, my son Bill, who flew the last bombing mission into Baghdad, would later become the Air Force (physician) Chief of Staff for Ramstein's Medical Facilities.
46 SGT. Brian Fahlstrom as quoted by Jacobsen, *A Story of the 311*[th] (p. 18)
47 Washington AP January 18, 1991

horizon. Civilian contractors some weeks later would supply us with air-conditioned huts that were similar to singlewide trailers. Lord only knows how much they cost. We left them on the hospital grounds when we departed.

From Jacobsen: "The day after we arrived we were informed that our duffel bags had been delivered to a flat area just outside of the hospital grounds. This area was to become our home for the duration of our stay. Tents were to be erected by the Red Crescent, the Islamic equivalent of the Red Cross."[48]

January 19: "Spent the next couple of days fighting the crud and getting the troops settled in. Tent City is coming along with Bedouin tents. Roman has dubbed it NODAK Dhabi."

January 20: "The 202nd has been virtually worthless as far as support goes. If it hadn't been for Air Force Col. Rust at Al Dhafra we would be in a world of hurt. Capt. D---- of the 202nd is carrying messages with threats to move individuals or our unit to a forward location, closer to the fighting, if we make waves. He tried to take back one of our vehicles today. I told him to go F---- himself. I got a call from his boss, Major A----, who was hostile, but we did not give in on the car; we gave him a bus instead. The situation regarding our financing and supplies is a nightmare. We are supposed to 'write the book.' I sent a fax to Livermore (Army Central Command) requesting supplies and a brief. They will arrive on Monday.

"Air strikes, (which) had started the night of January 16th-17th, were being continued around the clock. Got a brief from Col. Rust and watched 'packages' go out of Al Dhafra; F-16's. Tom

---

48 Jacobsen. *A Story of the 311*th (p. 20)

Rowekamp showed up this eve with our C-141 (supply flight). (They) had been held up in Germany when the war started."

The bottom line was that the supply flight finally landed at Al Dhafra AFB, UAE on January 20 around suppertime. SPC (Later SGT) Fahlstrom noted that during flight the uniform that everyone wore was BDU (Battle Dress Uniform). Full MOPP Gear was available at all times, but civilian clothes were required in the UAE.[49]

During the intense air assault against Iraq in the early part of the war, I sat in the operations center at Al Dhafra and listened to the communications during the tactical phase, which was going on twenty-four hours a day. New packages—meaning bombs and/or missiles—were being sent out every minute or so aboard fighter-bomber jets from all of the allied coalition forces around the clock. Someone in the operations staff later told me that we dropped more ordnance in tons in those few weeks than was dropped in Europe in all of WWII. I believed it when I got the after action reports of our EPW processing team and talked with the participants about the conditions of the enemy prisoners of war, who had been under the stress of constant around-the-clock bombing for weeks. They had hair and body lice. Their teeth were falling out. They had gastric and duodenal ulcers; alopecia, a condition where patches of hair fall out; scabies, a contagious skin disease caused by a mite that burrows under the skin; unattended wounds; injuries; and infections—just to name a few. None of them wanted to fight. Of course, we were unaware of this situation during the early days after our arrival. No one had the slightest inkling about how intensely the Coalition's strategic bombing and air assaults would be, and no-

---

49 Ibid-p19

body could predict the effect that these air assaults would have on the enemy and on our own medical resources.

January 20 (continued): "The perimeter defenses, which were sparse at first, now have five towers with thirty UAE Guards and concertina. They have .50 calibers, M-16's, and AKA's. Today we integrated our doctors with the local staff. The contract doctors are mostly Pakistanis, Indian, and Brits. I had a nice tour of the x-ray department with Dr. Gupta. Two CT Scanners, one in the ER

Dr. Gupta was the local staff contract Radiologist from India. In addition to myself, we also had Dr. Ed Faleski, a Radiologist in civilian life from Dickinson, North Dakota. Ed was a board-certified radiologist whom I knew. After the war, he would resign his civilian position and reenlist in the Air Force. I lost track of him after that.

"Our doctors will stay in the hospital by word of his Excellency Al Jaffa, who was a U.S.-trained surgeon, and the Deputy Minister of Health. He was a nice man. What a circus. The MedCom (Medical Commander) will be here tomorrow on January 21."

Monday, January 21: "The tent city is coming along. We are still trying to prepare for hot weather and we have ordered temper tents and caravans. The air strikes are continuing but there has been no significant ground action. I'm still fighting the Fort McCoy crud. A doctor and a troop commander got into fisticuffs. I called Jag at Al Dhafra for advice. I read the doctor his rights. He elected to be represented by a Jag officer. I appointed Col. Jacobsen as the investigating officer. The whole problem was later resolved with letters of reprimand, and we were able to avoid having anyone be court martialed.

I don't think the younger and junior officer had any inkling of the seriousness of striking another officer, especially in a combat zone. A prison sentence and dishonorable discharge was not out of the question from a legal standpoint, and some people on my staff were demanding a court martial. However, cooler heads prevailed and the combatants wound up settling their dispute by shaking hands.

January 21 (continued): "The staff meeting this a.m. was hilarious. Twenty people were in the room, phones were ringing, and beepers were going off. No one could determine whose mobile phone or beeper it was. I started taking antibiotics again because I have a deep cough. Lt. F---- is in the ICU with a possible MI (myocardial infarction). We have one air force patient with a ruptured L-3 vertebrae.

"S-4's (supply officers) from Higher Headquarters finally showed up. It sounds as if our supply problems are solved. We will have $250k to use for purchasing items on the local market, as well as push packages of class viii supplies.[50] The blood bank settled. We now have three military patients: one who was in a car accident, one who has ETOH (alcohol) toxicity, and a forty-two year old MI from our own unit."

Thursday, January 24: "Chaplain Stone locked up his mobile phone by pushing four numbers and the lock button. He found out that he couldn't unlock it if he didn't remember the numbers. Capt. Brooks (David O.) said we would have to call Japan to get a code or replace the memory chip, but he suggested that the code would likely be something simple like "1, 2, 3, 4." We tried it and—bingo—it unlocked!

---

50   *Wikipedia:* Army Class VIII Medical material (equipment and consumables) including repair parts.

Friday, January 25: "We continue to have mild glitches with communications. Higher Headquarters has a bad attitude. They have not helped us one iota. They continue to use threats and reference our complaints. They say, 'Either stop the 1539's (order requests) or we will send you to the front.' We now have documentation of their threats via their own fax, which was sent from some asshole named Major P----."

January 30: "Iraqi forces crossed the Saudi border on the 29th, and the probing ground action continues. So far, of the marines we've lost, eleven were KIA, two were MIA, and three were WIA."[51]

Above: Khafji is located just off Highway 95, below the border of Kuwait on the Gulf Coast. Note the position of Al Wafra to the northwest. Al Wafra, oil fields and a town in Kuwait, which would be a key point for U.S. Marines during the recapture of Khafji. Google Map modified by author.

51 The diary entry, from CNN's perspective, was also confirmed by Caryle Murphy and Guy Gugliotta of the Washington Post Foreign Service. Friday, February 1, 1991; Page A01. The 11 KIA were not all from Khafji, but other Iraqi probes as well.

THE BATTLE OF KHAFJI

I didn't know it at the time, but the above diary entry actually heralded what was likely the most significant battle of the Persian Gulf War: the Battle of Khafji, which took place between January 29 and 31 of 1991. As darkness fell on the eve of January 29, a column of between forty and fifty Soviet-made Iraqi tanks from Saddam's 3rd Armored Division approached the town of Khafji, which was located just south of the Kuwaiti-Saudi border on the Gulf Coast. The citizens of Khafji, which was in Saudi Arabia, had evacuated the town because they were nervous of possible artillery and rocket attacks, which actually occurred 2 hours after the Allied air assaults began on January 17th.[52] At this time a Coalition Force consisting of a U.S. transportation battalion, two U.S. Marine recon teams, and an unknown number of Saudi soldiers occupied it.[53]

The tanks approached the town with their turrets turned to the rear, an international signal of surrender. Behind the tanks, unseen by the town's defenders, was an estimated force of five hundred Iraqi soldiers loaded in vehicles from Iraq's 5th Mechanized Division. The defenders, observing the reversed turrets, allowed the tanks to approach, apparently anticipating an enemy surrender. When the Iraqis suddenly turned their turrets and opened fire, the defenders were caught off guard. In a very short time the Iraqis overwhelmed the defenders, established

---

52   Lowery, R.S., *Gulf War Chronicles* p-11
53   Grant, Rebecca and article by US Special Operations Command: www. specialoperations.com/memorial/spirit

an occupation force and made plans for defending a counter attack.[54]

Two soldiers from the U.S. transportation battalion, which included the 233rd Transportation Company, were listed as MIA in this action and captured by the Iraqis. One was the first female to be captured in Desert Storm, Army Specialist Melissa Rathbun-Nealy, a driver with the 233rd, and the other was fellow driver, Specialist David Locket. Both would later report that they were well treated, and they were released on March 6, 1991 after the surrender.

The six-man and seven-man marine reconnaissance teams were

Above: Melissa Rathbun-Nealy at a rally in her hometown of Grand Rapids, Michigan. [Photo credit: Grand Rapids Public Library]

able to avoid capture, and they took concealed positions on rooftops. One team, commanded by Corporal Charles H. Ingraham, found good observation posts on top of a three-story building, and the other team, commanded by Corporal Lawrence M. Lentz, found similar positions on other rooftops. Both recon teams would relay vital information on Iraqi positions during the subsequent battle.

---

54 Ibid page 2.

The reasons that the Battle of Khafji became so significant, according to Major Jeffrey B. Rochelle[55], were at least fourfold:

1. No other single battle in Desert Storm is significant for operational air power.

2. It exploited precision designed attack and surveillance systems in halting a major enemy offensive.

3. Air and ground forces were able to stop the enemy from large-scale movements and abandon their weapons.

4. The air power allowed the Coalition to reoccupy Khafji with extraordinarily few casualties.

Perhaps there was another good reason for its significance. The Battle of Khafji would turn out to be the only major offensive action by Iraq in the entire Gulf War, but it came at an awkward moment for the Coalition. "Stormin' Norman," General Norman H. Schwarzkopf, was in the midst of a three-week redeployment of his troops from the coastal area to attack positions about two hundred miles to the west. He was planning an end run around the Republican Guard, Saddam's elite infantry. Whether he was lucky or not, the situation forced Schwarzkopf to make what was likely his best decision of the war.

Rather than counter attack with his mobile assets, Schwarzkopf instructed his force commanders to use their air assets as the key element, along with U.S. Marines, Saudi National Guard

---

55 Rochelle is a USAF F-16 pilot with close to 3000 hours in the fighter; his opinions are from a graduation thesis for the School of Advanced Air Power Studies, Maxwell AFB, Al, 1997.

and other Coalition ground forces, primarily from Qatar to stop the attack.[56]

Air operations in the combat zone involved kill boxes, which were thirty-kilometer square grids on a map subdivided into four quadrants. "Planners pushed a four-ship flight through each kill box every seven to eight minutes in daytime and every fifteen minutes at night. In the designated area of the box, a flight leader was free to attack any targets he could identify.[57] Therefore, it was easy for Air Operations commanders to direct flight sorties into the kill boxes surrounding Khafji. Schwarzkopf had also directed his marines and the Saudi forces that were not surrounded, to positions twenty kilometers away from this particular kill box to allow for air assaults on Iraqi reinforcements without endangering Coalition ground forces. Marine forward air controllers were quick to interdict Iraqi forces attempting to reach Khafji.

Along with AC-130 gunships, A-10's and A-6's were scrambled as well as those aircrafts already diverted from other scheduled sorties, and they were very successful. One A-10 pilot named Captain Rob Givens was quoted later by Rebecca Grant and later recalled with some amazement: "I, myself—one captain in one airplane—was engaging up to a battalion size of armor on the ground and keeping these guys pinned for a little bit."[58]

---

56   Grant, Rebecca and article by US Special Operations Command: www.specialoperations.com/memorial/spirit p3.
57   Ibid. p. 4
58   Ibid.

Above: The A-10 Intruder[59] is similar to the one flown by Captain Rob Givens in the Battle of Khafji. Also called the Thunderbolt, the Fairchild-Republic A-10 is a single-seat twin-engine jet aircraft designed to provide close air support (CAS) of ground forces by attacking tanks, armored vehicles, and other ground targets. As a secondary mission, it provides airborne forward air control, guiding other attack aircraft against ground targets. It is the first US Air Force aircraft designed exclusively for close air support (CAS) of ground forces. The official nickname comes from the P-47 Thunderbolt of World War II, a plane that was particularly effective at the CAS mission. However, the A-10 is more commonly known as Warthog or simply Hog. In the USAF inventory, the same airframe is also designated OA-10 when used primarily in a forward air control role.[60] The more recent version of the A-10 is expected to remain in service until 2028. Photo credit footnote 59 below.

According to Colonel Terry Brosseau, retired executive officer of the 311th and Viet Nam combat veteran and advisor, the AC-130 gunships, which were called "Spooky" or "Spectre" were also extremely effective as close air support, and the Viet Cong and AVN were deathly afraid of them. The same was true of the Iraqis. The gunships armament consisted of 40mm and 105mm cannons and 25mm Gatling guns. In addition to its normal nine crew members, the gunship had five aerial gunners.

59 http://www.af.mil/information/factsheets/factsheet.asp?id=70
60 http://www.youtube.com/watch?v=zhPwaApe4Rk

Below: The A-6 version of the Thunderbolt or Warthog was retired in 1997.

Photo credit: Wikipedia

Above: The AC-130[61] gunship Spooky. Spooky's primary missions involve close air support, air interdiction, and force protection. Missions in close air support involve troops in contact, convoy escorts, and urban operations. Air interdiction missions are conducted against preplanned targets or targets of opportunity. Force protection missions include air base defense and facilities defense. Photo credit: http://www.airforceworld.com/attacker/eng/ac130-usaf-1.htm

---

61   http://www.af.mil/information/factsheets/factsheet.asp?fsID=71

Schwarzkopf's priorities were to stop Iraq from reinforcing the town and to recapture it while continuing to redeploy his troops for the surprise end run. The Marine commanders moved their charges into a position just south of Al Wafra in order to hold that sector, while the gunships, Cobra helicopters, and fixed wing aircraft virtually destroyed the Iraqi armor and vehicles. "The net effect was to strip the enemy of its ability to achieve surprise, momentum, massed effects, and dominance that are the hallmarks of successful maneuver."[62]

One impressive air attack on an approaching column of reenforcing Iraqi tanks was accomplished by disabling the lead and rear tanks with bombs, which trapped the rest of the column in between them. The attacking Coalition aircraft then systematically destroyed the entire column of some fifty tanks, which were left smoldering on the road, abandoned by their surviving crews. By late morning on January 31, the entire Iraqi offensive in Khafji had unraveled.[63]

Although the allied air campaign at Khafji was highly successful—easily the deciding factor for ending the Khafji conflict—the recapture of the town by necessity required boots on the ground, and that was not so easy. The Saudis demanded that they take the lead, and since it was their country, Schwarzkopf and the Coalition agreed. Each of the U.S. Marine recon teams were on rooftops about seven hundred meters apart, but surrounded by the enemy. Unseen by the Iraqis the Marines were critical in acting as forward artillery observers

---

62 : www.specialoperations.com/memorial/spirit p 5.
63 Ibid. p. 6

and directing fire. The Saudi and Qatari forces, however, had no decent communications with each other and their attacks were uncoordinated. After multiple attempts, and with support of U.S. Marine artillery, the SANG (Saudi Arabia National Guard) units and Qatari Infantry were able to secure the town, which was declared secured on February 1. A total of forty-three Coalition soldiers were KIA, fifty-two were WIA, and two were captured.[64] The Iraqis had over one hundred soldiers KIA, and about four hundred were captured.[65] Of the allied casualties, twelve of them were U.S. Marines, as reported by the BBC.[66] Another fourteen Coalition soldiers who were KIA were all from the USAF Gunship *Spirit 03*, which was commanded by Maj. Paul J. Weaver and hit by a handheld SAM (Surface to Air Missile). All fourteen crewmembers were killed when the AC-130 crashed into the Persian Gulf.[67]

Multiple military analysts would later agree that Saddam's intentions were to take charge of the Saudi Oil fields with his three infantry divisions and armor, which included the Republican Guard. He was, after all, the most powerful military force in the Middle East. U.S. and Allied Air Power, however, controlled the skies, and the Iraqi Air Force had been defeated in less than two weeks. Saddam was never able to use his ground forces effectively after that.

---

64 *Wikipedia*
65 U-Tube
66 http://news.bbc.co.uk/onthisday/hi/dates/stories/january/30/newsid_2506000/2506001.stm
67 www.specialoperations.com/Memorial/spirit.html

CHAPTER 5
FEBRUARY 1, 1991–FEBRUARY 16, 1991. Tent City, Medevac Flights, First North Dakota Gulf War Casualty

Too bad people can't always be playing music. Maybe then there wouldn't be any more wars. —**Margot Benary-Isbert, Rowan Farm**

*F*riday, February 1: *"Our setup in Tent City, which Col. Roman dubbed Camp Nodak Dhabi, is progressing nicely. Chaplains Stone and Nabben and Top (the 311ᵗʰ top kick, First Sergeant Jeffrey W. Campbell) have done an excellent job. We now have basketball, volleyball, table tennis, horseshoes, videos, TV, etc. and we are selling ice cream, beer, and soft drinks. I bought two pairs of civilian utility jeans for $6 each—a nice supplement to our civvies requirement.*

"We have a real problem communicating within our own organization due to a lack of "bleepers" (the contract doctors threw in an 'L' for what the Yanks called "beepers"). Locals are nervous about disaster drills.

Photo Above: Chemical Lab Specialist Sgt Ed Kenoly in his Arab dishdasha (casual robe) and keffiyeh (headdress also called a shmagh or a ghutrah) enjoying the Mafraq Saloon with Colonel Hook in his Mafraq civvies. Kenoly's keffiyeh is secured by a wreath called a tagiyyah.

Photo Below: RN 1st LT Gail Braaten, Radiologist LTC Ed Faleski, and Ophthalmologist Col. Gary Peterson. Author's photos.

Above: left to right, Chaplains Assistants Spc. Tamie Anderson (now Gerntholz), Tammy Ruhnke (now Nelson), and Chaplains 1st LT Dale Nabben, Major Nelson Stone. Photo credit Jacobsen.

Above: Duet singers Registered Nurse, Major Marci Lupien (now Ketterling) on the left and Pharmacy Specialist SSG Kathy Perkerewicz in their Mafraq civvies. Their favorite songs were "From a Distance" and "Winds Beneath My Wings." Photo by Jacobsen.

Sunday, February 3: "I spent last evening in a sing along to the accompaniment of Major Marcia Yonker Lupien (now Ketterling) and Loomis (refers to SFC Larry Loomis) on guitars. It didn't sound too bad!

The 311th had a number of other talented musicians, such as vocalist SSG Kathy Perkerewicz, keyboardist LTC Helen Johnson, and flute player Captain Melodee Grenz. There were many others as well. Lupien and Perkerewicz were particularly effective at singing duets in harmony.

February 3rd (continued) "One of our senior nurses wanted the men of the unit to have to wear long pants in the tent area since women were not allowed to wear shorts per local custom. I put a stop to that real quick, but I did negotiate with Dr.Gohary, Mafraq's Chief of Staff, to allow the girls to wear shorts in the tent area—at least until we get a complaint from the host nation Arabs. We'll see how it goes. First Sergeant Campbell, released a basic load of condoms, which made for some smart comments like, 'Where is the ration card?'

"The Mafraq Saloon beer garden opened with much success tonight. The troops seem to be really enjoying themselves. The day was marred by reports of minor thefts."

On February 4, 1991, as I was relaxing after a routine day of hospital administration, I happened to be sitting by myself in an alcove near my office/room watching television, which was tuned in to the usual CNN World News channel. When the news anchor reported that a B-52 had gone down in the Gulf and three of the crewmembers were missing, my anxiety level took a sudden pitch upward. I knew my son Bill had been deployed, but I had no clue where he was or what he was doing. I was pretty sure there was some mention of the missing members' home states, but no names were released. When I heard someone say, "North Dakota" my heart skipped a beat and my eyes filled with tears.

I was thinking, "What are the odds?" North Dakota had a population of only about six hundred thousand people, and the whole state surely had only a few natives in B-52 crews in spite of having Air Force Bases at Grand Forks, and Minot.

Around this time, Jim Miller, my executive officer and 1ˢᵗ Sergeant Jeff Campbell, came looking for me and caught me in emotional distress. Although their words were reassuring, it was a couple of days before I knew that my oldest son was safe. I then felt guilty and remorseful because I knew exactly how those families of the lost crewmen were feeling.

On February 4, 1991, the Associated Press published an article in several North Dakota newspapers concerning the first death of a North Dakota serviceman in the Gulf War. It was Air Force navigator Jeffry J. Olson from Grand Forks. His B-52 had gone down in the Indian Ocean while he was returning to base from a bombing run over Iraq.[68]

The report noted that military officials blamed the B-52 crash on mechanical problems and that of the six-man crew, two others lost their lives and three were rescued from the water.

Olson was a 1981 graduate of Grand Forks Red River High School and the U.S. Air Force Academy of Colorado Springs, CO. He was survived by his parents, retired Lt. Col. Norris Olson and his wife Jean, Jeff's mother, who reside in Grand Forks; his brother Marc, a B-52 pilot stationed in Minot, North Dakota; his wife, Cheryl, of Blytheville, Arkansas; his sister, Tara, of Moor-

---

68 (AP) *Bismarck Tribune.* February 4, 1991

head, Minnesota; and his grandmother, Alma Lierbo, of Minot. Jeff's dad, LTC Norris Olson had also been a B-52 pilot.

On October 27, 2012 I received this reply from Jeff Olson's mother after requesting permission to print his picture, and asking for more information about this heroic family:

Norris (Jeff's father) was in the first graduating class at the Air Force Academy in 1959. Marc (Jeff's older brother) graduated from the Air Force Academy in 1983 and Jeff graduated from the Air Force Academy in 1986. Jeff was on the prestigious Wings of Blue parachute team at the academy. All three of them obtained their Master's Degrees: Norris from the Air Force Institute of Technology: Marc from the University of Michigan, and Jeff from the University of Arkansas (not to be left out, I have my master's and doctorate from The University of North Dakota and our daughter graduated from Concordia, a private Lutheran college, and she has her Master's Degree from St. Thomas, St. Paul, Minnesota). The guys followed their father's choice and Tara teaches gifted children.

At the time of the Gulf War, Marc was an aircraft commander (AC) who flew B-52's—the H model out of Minot, North Dakota. Only the G models went to Diego.

This was an incredibly difficult time for us. After the accident, Marc was grounded for a time (surviving son bit).

It has been, if I may say, bittersweet to reflect on this; bitter for our loss of our son, Jeff, but sweet to remember what a fine human being he was and how blessed we were to have him in our lives.

Keeping positive thoughts and warm,

Jean[69]

---

69   Jean Olson, personal correspondence, 2012.

Olson's B-52 crashed while returning to Diego Garcia, the same Indian Ocean island base from which Bill Hook would fly

the last bombing mission over Baghdad in the Persian Gulf War just over three weeks later.

Tuesday, February 12: A lot has happened in the last ten days. We had a visit from the 202nd (our higher headquarters), which was at the very least unsatisfactory. Colonel Boatright and the gang bitched about there being too many requests, cars, phones, etc. We responded calmly enough but we were pissed. The next day we had a visit from U.S. Central Command, who had an Army representative, a Navy representative, and an Air Force representative. They were impressed with what we have accomplished with no help—especially the Air Force MASF (Mobile Aeromedical Staging facility). At the Air Force's suggestion, we renamed it AMEF for Army Medical Evacuation Facility.

Capt. Jeff Olson. Photo provided by Jeff's parents, LTC and Mrs. Norris Olson. Grand Forks, North Dakota.

The above-mentioned facility was part of our mission, and it was assigned to LTC Karen Eberhardt, one of the FNG's who was originally from Aurora's 5502nd U.S. Army Hospital. As I stated in my after action report, "She took the ball, ran with it, and performed magnificently."[70] I recommended her for a Bronze Star, but Higher Headquarters downgraded it to an Army Commendation Medal. At any rate, the facility was

---

70 Hook After action report.P15-16.

retained and used effectively when we started to get combat casualties, whereas the Air Force had previously planned to abandon it.

In my February 12 diary entry, talking about Central Command's visit, I wrote, "The best dude was Commander Hora of the Navy."

When I expressed reservations about complaining about our Higher Headquarters, I distinctly remember Commander Hora telling me, "What are they gonna do? Send you to Saudi Arabia?" joking about how we were already there. I relaxed after that and told him of our difficulties.

"We got along well and I let him know my feelings about the 202nd. Within forty-eight hours, Boatright was back with his chief nurse and a new attitude. I suspect someone got a chunk of his rear end."

Above: left to right, Central Command Medical Commander Col. D.G. Tsoulos, 311th Commander Col. Hook, 202nd Commander Col. Boatright. Tsoulos was a Viet Nam veteran who was known to a friend of mine from that conflict and said to be a good guy. Boatright and I repaired our fences and parted on fairly good terms at the end of the war. He actually gave me a set of Desert BDUs and awarded me an Army Commendation Medal. Author's Photo taken in Riyadh at Central Command HQ.

From the After Action Report: "Our problems with Higher HQ were attributed directly to the knowledge and attitude of the S-3 (operations) and S-4 (supply) officers. Once the communications difficulties and problems were made known to the 202nd Commander through Central Command, he acted quickly and decisively to correct them and we experienced no further problems concerning money."[71]

Also from the after action report: "Early on [in January] we were asked by the Air Force to supplement their limited number of flight surgeons on C-130 Medevac missions. Eighteen of our twenty-one doctors, including the commander, volunteered for this duty, and with the approval of higher headquarters we flew

---

71   Hook, After Action Report, p-19.

enough missions for everyone to go at least once. Before and after the start of the ground war the missions included transporting and caring for war wounded."[72]

Tuesday, February 12 (continued): "Our doctors have been flying medevac missions for the Air Force with some excitement. LTC Virgil Hayden, an OB-GYN Surgeon in civilian life, and Col. Gerald Moyer, the 311th Chief of Professional Services, observed a SCUD missile being intercepted over King Khalid Military City, A Saudi Air Force Base in the middle of the desert, while they were on approach to landing. They all say that the preflight briefing is the best part."

According to Doctor Hayden's report: "These missions were arranged through the Air Force at Bateen. Since we could not wear our uniforms in the U.A.E., we had to take them with us. We also drew weapons and ammunition. This was a very important part of the stay in the U.A.E. The air bases in Saudi Arabia were collection points for war casualties, and this enabled me to see many parts of the land I would not have been able to see. I went to Jawal, which is the main base for the Stealth Fighter (F-117). During the medevac flights I was able to visit almost every air base in Saudi Arabia.

"Prior to leaving on these missions, we would have a security briefing by the Air Force. The information that was provided at that time gave us a much wider picture of what was going on in the war. At my first briefing, it became apparent that most of our ground forces were not stationed just south of Kuwait, as everyone had been led to believe, but there was a large concentration

___

72 Ibid, p-15.

of troops just south of the intersection of the Kuwait-Iraqi border. When the ground war started, 'Stormin Norman' was going to make an end run, just like Patton did in WWII.

"On one of the medevac flights, we were on final approach to King Khalid City Airport to pick up casualties, when all of a sudden the plane banked rapidly to the west and increased power. As I looked out the window, I saw two Patriot missiles take out a SCUD missile. I guess this event will stay with me forever. Because the base was on Red Alert, we were forced to circle for almost an hour. Once we landed we picked up our casualties. The pickup was made tactically, meaning that the engines were not stopped nor did the aircraft come to a full stop. One great thing about the medevac flights was being able to eat in Air Force mess halls where they served great American food.

"As we would fly from the U.A.E. on these missions, we flew below five thousand feet, which allowed us to have a bird's eye view of everything. We flew over the Empty Quarter several times. You would have to see it to believe how desolate it was. At other times when we flew over the Gulf, it would appear a beautiful shade of blue, reminding me of the Blue Lagoon of Hawaii. We also saw many of the oil wells in the Gulf."[73]

Tuesday, February 12 (continued): "I just got word this evening that I will be on tomorrow's medevac flight. We are apparently scheduled to go to the Saudi-Iraqi border above KKMC (King Khalid Military City). It makes me understandably apprehensive. If Linda knew about the risks, she would have a hissy fit. It gives one food for thought when you realize this could be the

73 Jacobsen. *A Story of the 311th* (p. 23-24) Quoting Dr. Hayden.

last night of mortal life, but like I've always said, 'No one gets out of the world alive.' I'll probably add more lines later and realize what a fool I was."

Above and below: Col. Hook with unnamed Air Force Flight Surgeon and Flight Nurse prior to leaving on medevac mission on Feb. 13, 1991..

Above: C-130 medevac mission aircraft at Bateen AFB. February 13, 1991. Pilot
Capt. McDaniel. Author's photo.

Friday, February 16 (three days after the February 13th mission): "Well, indeed I was foolish. The medevac flight turned out to be a milk run. We picked up our first case (a Marine with probable PTSD)[74] at a base north of KKMC (No sign of hostiles). Then we flew to Jeddah on the Red Sea. I was surprised to find a squadron of BUFFs (Big Ugly Fat F---ers—Air Force parlance for the B-52. Polite folks would call them Big Ugly Fat Fellows). We added three more ambulatory cases to our marine psych case and then flew to Riyadh. Before we left Jeddah, I talked with a psychologist attached to the AF Tactical Hospital. He told me that the Saudis in Jeddah had beheaded in public one of the Palestinians who had led the terrorist attack on a bus last week. There was no trial. He also said that they

---

74 PTSD Post Traumatic Stress Disorder.

were under threatcon (threat condition) Charlie[75] too, but they had nice tent quarters on the beach and did a lot of snorkeling."

According to Google/Chrome Worldview 1991: "Despite the huge U.S. military presence in Saudi Arabia, there was only one act of terrorism directed against U.S. forces. On 3 February 1991, two U.S. airmen and a Saudi guard were wounded in an attack on a military bus in Jeddah. Four Palestinians (one a naturalized Saudi) and two Yemenis were arrested. The incident is still under investigation, and the four Palestinians remain in custody"[76] (This report apparently written before the beheading).

I also remember taking out my digital camera while we were in Jeddah. I was about to snap a picture of the B-52s when I felt a hand on my shoulder and I heard a voice say, "You'd better put that away, Colonel." Apparently, Jeddah was at that time a classified B-52 base. I wondered if my son Bill was there. I knew by then he had likely been deployed, but I did not know his location. It turned out he was at Diego Garcia in the Indian Ocean.

Friday, February 16 (continued): "I talked with the C-130 Pilot, Captain McDaniel, who trained at Columbus AFB, Mississippi, shortly before Bill. When he found out that my son was flying BUFFs, he invited me into the cockpit and gave me a set of earphones. It was a lot of fun listening to the chatter, particularly around Riyadh (That's when the flight engineer pointed out the missile-in flight mentioned in the Preface). We picked up three litter patients and four ambulatories in Riyadh and dropped off

---

75 Threatcons ranged from A, the lowest, to D, the highest (threat is imminent).

76 http://www.fas.org/irp/threat/terror_91/mideast.html

our Marine who had PTSD. We then flew to Bahrain and dropped all of our patients. There were no patients for us in Abu Dhabi this time. Riyadh had a nice MASF (Mobile Air Staging Facility) or AMEF (Army Medical Evacuation Facility) set up with coffee and donuts etc. I am very impressed with the AF Flight Nurses. C-130s are very noisy but efficient. Twelve hours of flight time."

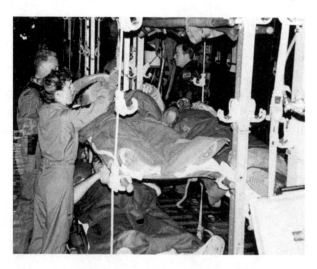

Above: Flight nurses and medics care for the casualties that are being transferred from Riyadh to Bahrain on February 13, 1991. Each flight carried several nurses and medics and two physicians. Although the Allied ground offensive had not yet started the Coalition forces were experiencing combat casualties from Iraqi probes, missiles, and other incidents like the one that had occurred at Khafji. Author's photo.

Saturday, February 16: "We had a Valentine's Day party on Thursday the 14th. Al Dhafra AFB responded with a party on Friday. I didn't go but some of our young troops got drunk. One girl fell off the bus kissing her date goodnight. Bateen's reciprocal barbecue dance is tomorrow, Sunday."

CHAPTER 6
FEBRUARY 24, 1991–FEBRUARY 27 1991. Tanks and Battles, Scuds and Social Intercourse

Battles are won by slaughter and maneuver. The greater the general, the more he contributes in maneuver, the less he demands in slaughter —**Winston Churchill**

Sunday, February 24: "Another week has gone by. With lots of rhetoric and diplomacy, the Soviets and the Iraqis tried to play games by agreeing to an unconditional withdrawal, which of course had lots of conditions. I was proud of Bush for not buying it, and the ground assault started about 0430 this morning. Secretary of Defense Cheney has blocked out the news, but some bits and pieces are coming over CNN.

"We finally received our Medical Supply Push packages, so I reported us as "Mission Ready." The only thing we're lacking is orthopedic internal fixation devices, such as intramedullary rods and screws. I talked with Col. Boatright this morning and he continues to have a cooperative attitude.

"Last night we had the social intercourse dinner with Dr. Amin Gohary and his administrative staff."

I had had a meeting with Dr. Amin Al Gohary, Mafraq's Chief of Staff, some days before and we had discussed how well the integration of the two staffs was going. He had suggested that perhaps our two administrative staffs could get together in some sort of social gathering to celebrate, and I agreed that "social intercourse" was a good idea. As soon as I said the words I knew it was a mistake. Dr. Gohary's reaction was immediate and alarming. It took me several minutes to explain that I was not suggesting some sort of group sex party, but after I got him settled down we both envisioned a waiting line to join in, on both sides of the aisle. Needless to say, my comment made for a few laughs.

"We had lots of laughs about his initial Egyptian interpretation of "social intercourse." The party was held on a yacht that was moored in the Gulf. Both the military and civilian administrations sat on cushions on the deck, and we ate with our fingers. The banquet was marvelous. They served a magnificent dinner of several courses, including the traditional fatted lamb, endless shrimp kabobs, fruit, dates, Arab tea, and coffee. Everything was served while we were sitting on the floor. A bus then took us to the Abu Dhabi Sheraton, where we Americans had a couple of drinks. I slept well and awoke to find that the ground war was in full force. I wrote up Loomis's story about overthrowing the government for the Daily Bulletin to be published the next day (note: I can't find a copy and don't remember the story).

Because the ground offensive, which was about to start, primarily involved the armored U.S. Forces of the VII Corps and armored elements of Great Britton's 1st Division, and the technological best of these units were the Abram's M1-A1 tank and its British Counterpart, the Challenger, I will introduce some data on these weapons. I will start with an interview with an Abram's Tank Platoon Commander and instructor, 1st Lieutenant Paul F. Hook, to give the reader some idea of the ability of these weapons and how they were used in 1991.

Lt. Paul F. Hook, circa 1990

June 6, 2012 interview with Paul Hook regarding his military service:

WFH "Paul, you graduated from U. Cal Santa Barbara in—"

PFH "1988."

WFH "And you got your ROTC commission in '88?"

PFH "Yes."

WFH "And then after you got your commission you went directly into the service?"

PFH "I went directly to an Armor Officer Basic Course."

WFH "And when did you complete that?"

PFH "That was a sixteen-week course, so—"

WFH "So that was probably about September or October of '88?"

PFH "Thereabouts, yes."

WFH "So, tell me about the tank. Was it an Abrams?"

PFH "Yes—an Abrams M1-A1."

WFH "So tell me about it"

PFH   "Well, unloaded it weighs about sixty-two tons. It's driven by a General Electric gas turbine engine, which delivers 2500 horse power."

WFH   "What about the crew; how many?

PFH   "It has a four-man crew: a tank commander, a gunner, a loader/radio operator, and a driver."

WFH   "Tell me about the equipment on the tank. What can you see on your screen?

PFH   "Oh, basically looking through the sites of the Commander's viewer you see a crosshair, which has horizontal and vertical lines in a concentric circle, and since the gunnery sites are all computer-operated, all you have to do is put that circle on your target, hit a laser range finder, and since there is a device almost like a weather station on the tank itself that calculates the wind velocity and various atmospheric conditions—"

WFH   (interrupting) "Rotation of the earth and all that stuff?"

PFH   "Oh, yeah, all that stuff. So all you have to do is put that dot on the target, hit the laser range finder, and then you are ready to fire."

WFH   "What size shell do you use?"

PFH   "It's a 120mm shell. The gun has a smooth bore like a shotgun with no rifling at all and we fired a Sabot[77] round and a high explosive anti-tank round." (HEAT)

77

Photo above: Anti-tank Sabot armor-piercing round with its two matched spindles containing an armor piercing dart called a flechette. Sabots are used to fire the flechettes that form anti-armor kinetic energy penetrators.[78]

Photo below: The DU (depleted uranium) penetrator, right after leaving the gun[79]. Depleted uranium penetrators have a density two-and-a-half times greater than steel. Paul Hook says the penetrator "rattles around in the target tank and creates shrapnel. If it hits a fuel tank it will blow." The HEAT rounds are used primarily for other targets."[80]

---

78 Wikipedia
79 Ibid.
80 Paul Hook personal correspondence.

WFH   "What kind of range does it have?"

PFH   "It could reach four thousand meters, which is four kilometers." (2.48 miles)

WFH   "That's a long ways out there. That's out there about two and a half miles isn't it?"

PFH   "Close. Yeah, it could reach out and touch someone."

WFH   "Ok, then tell me, after you were sent to your Armor outfit where did they deploy you or where did you go next?"

PFH   "Once I received my final unit orders I was sent to Schweinfurt, Germany."

WFH   "And your unit was?"

PFH   "The 3rd Infantry Division, 1st Brigade, in what was then the 2nd battalion, 64th Armor Regiment. It has since been re-designated."

WFH   "So, how many tanks did you have in your brigade?"

PFH   "In the brigade, there were 104, which were in two battalions."

WFH   "That's a good sized armored brigade."

PFH   "Yes, one battalion at maximum strength had fifty-eight tanks."

WFH   "So, you were commissioned a 2nd Lieutenant. Did you get any promotions after that?"

PFH   "Yes, I did. I was promoted to 1st Lieutenant and I served in a support platoon. My first assignment was in Delta Company, 3rd Platoon."

WFH   "And that was an armored company?"

PFH   "Yes, that was an M1-A1 Abrams Tank Company."

WFH   "So, you were a tank commander then?"

PFH   "I was a tank commander and a tank platoon leader, so I was responsible for not only my own tank but three other tanks as well."

WFH   "Who was your senior commander then?"

PFH   "The ones I remember are LTC Gary Kreuger when I arrived and LTC Bill Henricksen followed him."

WFH   "You mentioned to me that the Division Commander and General Schwarzkopf did not get along."

PFH   "Yes, I did. My recollection is that—"

WFH   (interrupting) "Was there some reason for that?"

PFH   "There were political considerations that existed between the two men that resulted in the 3rd Infantry Division not being deployed from Germany for Desert Storm. However, we did have many units within the 3rd Division deploy to the Middle East as individual sub units."

WFH   "Where were you when Desert Shield became Desert Storm?"

PFH   "Well, it's interesting. When Bill was about to be deployed, I heard he was in California for some reason. I was still training in Germany about thirty-five kilometers from the Czech border. I remember wondering what he was doing out there."

WFH   "We'll have to ask him, but I think he was instructing other B-52 pilots just before he went overseas, and he was probably on a training flight out there."

Note: Bill was flying the H model B-52s before being deployed. The H models were a bit different than the G models that were being used in the Persian Gulf War. In January of 1991, both models were nuclear weapon capable, but the H model was a technical upgrade. In a later conversation, Bill explained that he was out in California at Castle AFB, in Merced, California, to get refreshed on the older G model B52 before being deployed.

WFH   "And when did you finally get out of the service?"

PFH   "In May of '92."

WFH   "So, you really served for nearly four years after college."

PFH   "That's right."

WFH   "Was that your obligation?"

PFH   "Yes, that was my full obligation."

WFH   "Tell me about your most dynamic experience with the Armored Platoon."

PFH   "That's kind of tough. About every six months we had a training mission to go out on. We had two rotations. One was to Grafenwoehr where we conducted Tank qualifications. So we would go to the range and run what is known as tank tables. And you have Tank Table Eight, which are individual crew qualifications. And as platoon leader, I would have to run what is known as Tank Table Twelve, which is a Platoon qualification. On my very first attempt to qualify on Tank Table Eight, I shot what would have been a perfect score had it not been for a misfired coaxial machine gun. That problem cost us about ninety-two points. So, we ended up with

908 out of a thousand—one thousand being a perfect score."

WFH   "You had some experience training other tank crews, did you not?"

PFH   "That is correct. Actually, during Desert Storm our unit was deployed to Grafenwoehr and we set up a training mission where units from the U.S. would come in to Germany prior to being sent on to the combat zone and we would train them for two weeks."

WFH   "I know that when we went for pre-deployment training we wound up with just over two weeks of training in the snow only to go to the desert, which made a lot of sense (laughter). I suppose the same thing happened with you guys, you know, at that time in December and January 1990 and the war broke out as I recall about the middle of January of '91."

PFH   "You know, I still have all the *Stars and Stripes* issues from that time."

WFH   "I'd like to see those. If you could loan those to me, it would help in putting this story together."

PFH   "Sure, I can do that."[81]

WFH   "It would also help if you can write down some dates if you can remember. Anything else that you can tell me as far as what your life was like in those days and where you felt that you were as far as your military

---

81   Paul did. See references later in the text.

experience—whether you liked it and so forth and so on."

PFH   "Those were very interesting times. My feelings were like an alternating electric current. I would go from having the best job in the world to wondering at times why the heck I was doing it. Then I would think that what I was doing was absolutely terrible."

WFH   "Did you ever get concerned about your brother being in the combat zone?"

PFH   "No, as far as you or Bill, I never felt anxiety over that."

WFH   "I did—for all of us, I guess. I never knew when or if either of you would be deployed at first. The worst experience that I had concerning Bill involved CNN. You know your brother Chris used to call army intelligence an oxymoron. There was no such thing as intelligence as far as we were concerned unless we traveled several miles to one of the Air Force bases to seek out information. So, most of the information concerning what was happening came over CNN and we did have television. It was like having cell phones—only better—and we could talk to anybody in the world with the phones. We could listen to all of the global news. I don't remember the date, but it was in February of '91 when one of our B-52's went down. I knew Bill had been deployed and was over there someplace, but I didn't know where."

PFH   "And that caused some anxiety?"

WFH   "Well, it might not have been so bad, but CNN reported that a kid from North Dakota had been lost. And it turned out to be a true story. He was a navigator on the B-52 that went down. He was originally from Fargo, then later Grand Forks, and he had been deployed out of Eaker AFB, Arkansas. And he got killed."

PFH   "Oh Dear!"

WFH   "Yeah, it was kind of a scary day, and there were a couple of more bad days until I found out that Bill was safe. Well, thank you very much. I'll get this down on paper; try to make some sense of it."

PFH   "Yes those were some memorable times. Do you remember when the Berlin Wall came down? I was on border patrol then. I actually have a mug celebrating the event, but I will have to look at it to be sure."

WFH   "I don't remember exactly either."

Monday, February 25: "I got a call from Boatright with a heads-up for a possible further deployment. We are supposed to anticipate a forty-eight-hour notice. He gave me no specific information. I speculate that we will go to Kuwait City once it is secured. Wouldn't you know it? We were just getting comfortable with caravans, which are air conditioned huts which are not all in yet. A SCUD hit Dhahran last night, killing twenty-seven US troops, and there are over ninety WIA. The unit has not been identified in the news."

"At 8:40 pm (12:40 pm EST) on February 25, 1991, parts of an Iraqi SCUD missile destroyed the barracks housing members of the National Guardsmen.[82] The unit, the 14th Quartermaster Detachment, was an Army Reserve water purification unit stationed in Greensburg, Pennsylvania.[83]

"In the single most devastating attack on U.S. forces during that war, twenty-eight soldiers died and ninety-nine were wounded. The 14th Quartermaster Detachment lost 13 soldiers and suffered forty-three wounded. Casualties were evacuated to medical facilities in Saudi Arabia and Germany.

"The 14th, which had been in Saudi Arabia for only six days, suffered the greatest number of casualties of any allied unit during Operation Desert Storm. Eighty-one percent of the unit's sixty-nine soldiers had been killed or wounded."[84]

From the internet: "On February 24, a massive coalition ground offensive began, and Iraq's outdated and poorly supplied armed forces were rapidly overwhelmed. By the end of the day, the Iraqi Army had effectively folded, ten thousand of its troops were held as prisoners, and a U.S. air base had been established deep inside Iraq."[85]

Here are some of the weapons:

---

[82] Although there may have been National Guard housed in the barracks, the unit that suffered the most was an Army Reserve water purification unit from Greensburg, PA.
[83] http://www.qmfound.com/14th_Quartermaster_Detachment.htm
[84] http://www.history.com/this-day-in-history/gulf-war-ground-offensive-begins
[85] ibid

M1 -A1 HA (Heavy Armor) Abrams, 3rd Armored Cavalry Regiment "Brave Rifles" Desert Storm, 1991.[86]

"The driver sits in the front center in a semi-reclining position when his hatch is closed. He steers with a motorcycle-type T-bar with twist grip controls for managing the throttle and electronic fuel. A panel displays the condition of the fluid levels, filters, batteries, electrical connectors, and circuit breakers. Opening to the right is the driver's single hatch, which has three integral periscopes. He has a 120-degree field of view. His night-driving periscope will fit into the loader's periscope housing.

"The commander and gunner sit on the right of the turret, and the loader is on the left. The commander has six periscopes that cover three hundred and sixty degrees. He also has an x3 sight

---

86   Photo Credit: http://www.fprado.com/armorsite/abrams.htm

for the fifty-caliber machine gun and an optical extension of the gunner's primary sight (GPS). This GPS has dual x10 and x3 day optics or x10 and x3 thermal imaging night vision, a Hughes laser rangefinder, and sight stabilization. The gunner has an x8 auxiliary sight. The loader has an x1 periscope that can traverse 360°."[87]

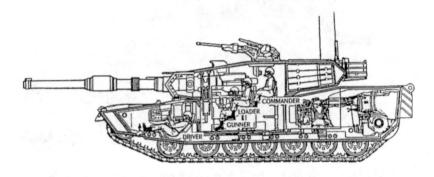

Above: M1-A1 side view

Some interesting components of the Abrams include a gas tank that holds 504.4 gallons of fuel. Like most military vehicles, it can burn diesel, automotive gasoline, or jet fuel (kerosene). It has a range of 298 miles, it burns three hundred gallons every eight hours, and it has a maximum governed speed of forty-two mph. Its cross-country speed is thirty mph. It has a fording depth without a kit of four feet and it can climb a four-foot wall. Its armor is classified.[88] The tank's most serious rival in Gulf War I was the outdated Russian-manufactured T-72, yet the Abrams had twice the effective firing range, better armor, better ammo, and better technology—not to mention better trained crews.

---

87   ibid
88   http://www.inetres.com/gp/military/cv/tank/M1.htm

Military-Today.com

Above: The British Challenger 1. The Challenger 2 has since replaced it.

The British Challenger 1 was similar to the Abrams M1-A1. It too was armed with the 120-mm cannon, but with a rifled barrel. It was a more sophisticated version than its predecessor, the Chiefton. It had a dual-plane stabilizer. Most of the combat load consisted of armor-piercing sub-caliber rounds, including those with depleted uranium alloy core. The fire control system included a laser sight-range finder and an electronic ballistics computer. The commander's periscopic sight had a stabilized field of vision that was linked with the gunner's main sight. Challenger tanks were outfitted with an infrared sight for the gunner."[89]

---

89   http://www.globalsecurity.org/military/world/europe/challenger1.htm

Above: The U.S. Bradley armored personnel carrier/ fighting vehicle.

In an article written by Charles Babcock of *The Washington Post* and published in *Stars and Stripes*,[90] Babcock lauded the effectiveness of Abrams M1-A1 tanks on the desert battlefields, especially over the Iraqi Soviet-made T-72. He also quoted such experts on Soviet armor as David Isby, who indicated that the Abram's better optics and computer far surpassed the T-72 in long-range accuracy and night warfare. Babcock also effectively described the use of sabot armor-piercing rounds that I previously noted, calling them dense metal arrows that travel up to a mile per second.

Tuesday, February 26: "No word from Boatright today. Rumor control is out of hand following a press conference-like (question and answer) session with our section leaders."

---

90   *Stars and Stripes* Vol. 49, No. 318, February 28, 1991 P1.

Wednesday, February 27: "202nd called back with word to 'gear up' but only on a contingency basis. They confirmed that if re-deployment does happen it will most likely be Kuwait City. Rumors continue with the Fargo section, which as usual is out of control." Of the three sections of the 311th, Bismarck, Fargo and Minot, Fargo— God Bless 'em—was the most creative in the rumor mill.

THE BATTLE OF BUSAYYAH: FEBRUARY 26, 1991:

Just before dawn on February 26, 1991, near the Iraqi town of Al Busayyah, the 2nd Brigade—known as the "Iron Brigade" of the U.S. 1st Armored Division (1AD), part of VII Corps, commanded by General Frederick M. Franks, Jr.—approached a crossroads defended by eleven dug-in Iraqi tanks, twelve other armored vehicles, multiple machinegun nests, and selected fighting positions around the town. Trenches stretched several hundred meters south of town, radiating out to perimeter strong points, and there were other vehicles and at least one more tank in the vicinity.[91]

It was a small village of only about fifty buildings. The Iraqi defenders included about four hundred infantry soldiers, a small unit of Iraqi commandos, and the reinforced armored units noted above. As the American units crossed the Iraqi line designated "Phase Line Smash," mortars dropped smoke rounds on the Iraqi forward positions, which resulted in the Iraqi defenders almost immediately surrendering.

To make a long story short, the bottom line was: "As the task force swept through the objective, the brigade ordered the battalion to expeditiously move north in order to clear a kill box for an in-

---

91 http://en.wikipedia.org/wiki/Battle_of_Al_Busayyah

coming artillery strike on the town. Persistent resistance from within the town had prompted the artillery barrage. The main body was able to move quickly, but trail elements handling prisoners of war delayed the fire mission. At 0850 the box was clear and the artillery mission (called 'arty prep' by the troops) was executed. At this point the Iron Brigade continued to push northeast."[92]

The battle of Al Busayyah resulted in sixteen enemy soldiers captured and numerous vehicles including twelve tanks, two BRDMs,[93] one BMP,[94] and twenty-five wheeled vehicles destroyed. The U.S. 2nd Iron Brigade of the 1st Armored Division would go on to fight at the Battle of Medina Ridge the following day.

Above: Location of the small village of Al Busayyah well into Iraqi territory. Google Map modified by author.

---

92 Ibid.
93 BRDM Boyevaya Razvedyvatelnaya Dozornaya Mashina. A Soviet made 4 wheeled amphibious vehicle.
94 See photo page105.

Two Marines lower the trim vane on the front of an Iraqi BMP-1 IFV, an amphibious vehicle captured during Operation Desert Storm.[95]

THE BATTLE OF MEDINA RIDGE: FEBRUARY 27, 1991

In an article by Michael R. Gordon in the *New York Times* on April 8, 1991, Gordon described the desert where the 2nd armored Brigade of Iraq's Medina Division was annihilated as "an impressive tableau of destruction."[96] He also described seeing amid the rubble orange plastic markers where Americans had buried the Iraqi dead. The markers were few and far between because the Iraqi tanks had exploded and burned so quickly. Gordon quoted Col. Montgomery Meigs, Commander of the

95 http://en.wikipedia.org/wiki/File:Captured_Iraqi_BMP-1.jpg
96 http://www.nytimes.com/1991/04/08/world/after-the-war-gi-s-recall-destruction-of-powerful-iraqi-force.html

2nd Brigade (Iron Brigade), as saying, "It means there were not a whole lot of bodies."[97]

More than one hundred Iraqi tanks and armored personnel carriers were destroyed at the battle site about twenty miles from the northwest corner of Kuwait. The Iraqi Brigade was a part of the Republican Guard, Iraq's elite force. The battle lasted just forty minutes, but some described it as the largest and most confusing tank battle of the war (For a fascinating account from a soldier who was there, I refer the reader to a blog by Dan Welch on 12/19/98.[98] Medina Ridge would be NE of Busayyah between Busayyah and highway 8 on the previous map).

Schwarzkopf himself described his end run around Kuwait as a "left hook," but the actual boots-on-the-ground commander of the VII Corps was General Frederick M. Franks, Jr., a Viet Nam veteran who had lost his left leg fighting in Cambodia. This highly decorated combat seasoned officer was born in West Lawn, PA, and was a graduate of West Point, class of 1959. Just a year younger than me his curriculum vitae was impressive. His awards for valor included the Silver Star, the Bronze Star, two Purple Hearts, a DFC and an Air Medal. Highly respected by both his troops and his superiors, Franks had fought and succeeded to retain a combat command after his below-the-knee amputation.[99] Trained as both an armored

---

97 Ibid.
98 http://www.tanksim.com/topic14.htm
99 http://en.wikipedia.org/wiki/Frederick_M._Franks,_Jr.

officer and a ranger, Franks knew what was needed in combat to succeed.

From Wikipedia: "In early November, 1990, Franks was ordered to deploy the VII Corps to Saudi Arabia to join the international coalition preparing to drive Iraqi forces from Kuwait and on 24 February 1991, the Desert Storm land assault began, with VII Corps making the main attack. VII Corps consisted of 146,000 American and British soldiers in essentially five armored divisions (one was a mechanized infantry division and one was a cavalry division). This consisted of close to sixteen hundred American and British tanks, and eight hundred helicopters. Supporting this was its support command and vital logistics support command comprising over twenty-six thousand soldiers and fifteen hospitals. In total, VII Corps consumed over two million gallons of fuel a day. In one hundred hours of rapid maneuver and combat, VII Corps fought several engagements with Iraqi forces. Under Franks' leadership, VII Corps units gained decisive victories at the Battle of 73 Easting, the Battle of Norfolk, and the Battle of Medina Ridge."[100]

According to *Wikipedia*, Schwarzkopf publicly expressed some frustration over VII Corp's slow advance, which allowed some of the Republican Guard to escape capture or destruction during the advance. On February 27, the third day of the ground offensive, and late in the day at 2100 hours, Schwarzkopf ordered a cease-fire for the next day. He apparently did this without talking to Franks, who had stated that he needed another day to complete the job. The original order halted combat operations at

---

100 ibid

0500 on February 28, but was later extended to 0800. Whatever the controversy, the bottom line was that Franks, operating on his own timetable, secured "one of—if not THE—largest, fastest, most successful armor maneuvers in history."[101]

The *Wikipedia* writer also accused Schwarzkopf of extending "the FSCL (Fire Support Coordination Line) so far north and east that air interdiction of retreating Iraqi troops was impossible."[102] There is at least one research paper written about whether it is the Air Force's or the ground force's responsibility to establish the FSCL.[103]

Both generals (Franks was a three-star Lieutenant General and Schwarzkopf was a four-star General of the Army) have expressed their side of things in books; Franks tells the story in his own words in his and Tom Clancy's book *Into the Storm: On the Ground in Iraq*, which gives different opinions than those made by Schwarzkopf in his own autobiography, *It Doesn't Take a Hero*. As far as I am concerned, both men are national heroes and neither of them has disparaged the other in writing.

The two other tank battles of 73 Easting and Norfolk have been described extensively by those who were there, the descriptions of which are detailed on the internet as well as in books and theses. They affected the 311th only in the number of EPW's and the few battle casualties they produced, but they certainly put the icing on the end-of-the war cake.

An Easting is like a longitude line on a map. It was named for a UTM (Universal Transverse Mercator) north-south coordinate

---

101 Ibid
102 Ibid.
103 http://www.dtic.mil/dtic/tr/fulltext/u2/a398429.pdf

line and is readable on a GPS receiver in kilometers. The Mercator zone is six degrees of longitude wide, split by a central meridian line into east and west halves. To avoid negative numbers on the west side, any figure less than five hundred kilometers is known to be west of the central meridian.

THE BATTLE OF 73 EASTING:

The Battle of 73 Easting has been described as the last great tank battle of the Twentieth Century.[104] It was fought just a few hours after Busayyah on 26–27 February 1991. The Coalition Forces participating included VII Corps units of both American and British composition. The main U.S. Unit was the 2nd ACR (Armored Cavalry Regiment), a force of over ten thousand soldiers with three ground squadrons, an attack helicopter squadron, and a support squadron. The VII Corps included two American (the 1st and 3rd) and one British (the 1st) Armored Divisions and one American Infantry Division (the 1st known as Big Red One).[105]

When it was all over, the Coalition suffered one KIA and sixty-nine WIA, but fifty-seven of those were from friendly fire when one Bradley was destroyed. Iraq suffered anywhere from six hundred to one thousand or more KIA or WIA, and lost eighty-five tanks and forty armored personnel carriers.[106]

---

104 http://en.wikipedia.org/wiki/Battle_of_73_Easting
105 See appendix D for breakdown of units of the US Army.
106 http://en.wikipedia.org/wiki/Battle_of_73_Easting

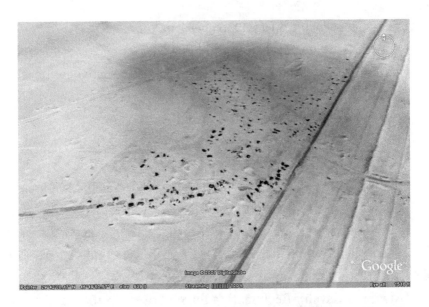

Above: The tank and armored personnel carrier graveyard of Iraqi Forces from the Battle of 73 Easting. Note the GPS coordinates in the lower left hand corner of the image. Google map source provided by John Clifford [107]

THE BATTLE OF NORFOLK:

Also fought on February 27, the Battle of Norfolk was described by *Wikipedia* as a continuation of the Battle of 73 Easting, which was fought 2Km. to the west. Units of Freddie Franks' VII Corps included two Brigades of Big Red One Infantry and the 3rd Brigade of the 2nd Armored Division. They also had support from one of Big Red One's attack Helicopter Battalions and the 4th Battalion of the 3rd Division Artillery. Their opponents were units of the Republican Guard, which included the Tawakalna

---

107 http://thirtysecondthoughts.blogspot.com/2007/02/anniversary-of-deci-sive-gulf-war-tank.html

Mechanized Infantry Division and the 37th Brigade of the 12th
Iraqi Tank Division.

In a foggy six-hour battle, Coalition Armor and Artillery
destroyed the Iraqi infantry division and Big Red One seized
Objective Norfolk. "American casualties were six soldiers
killed (all but one by friendly fire) and thirty wounded."[108]
The Iraqi casualties were not well documented but here is a
short blog from on February 26, 2012, written by a soldier
who was there and titled *21 Years Ago Tonight*:[109] Reprinted
with permission.

"February 26, 1991 was the date of what has been called 'the
last great tank battle of the twentieth century.' It's been known
as the Battle of 73 Easting. For us in the 1st Battalion/41st Infantry, it was Objective Norfolk. The actual battle began in the
late afternoon by the 2nd Armored Cavalry Regiment when they
made contact with elements of Iraqi Republican Guard and an
Armored Division and systematically reduced the units to scrap
heaps before we arrived on the scene at about 2 a.m. when we
passed through their forward lines and picked up the battle.

"There was a bit of confusion at our entrance into the battle,
which resulted in B Co. 1/41 (1st Battalion/ 41st Infantry Regiment) losing a platoon (three of their four Bradleys) to M1A1
fire. Like I said, earlier in the month, 1/41st had the highest casu-
alty rate of any infantry unit in the war because both sides were
shooting at us, the price we paid for being in the lead."[110]

108 http://www.tanksim.com/topic14.htm
109 Jonn Lilyea http://thisainthell.us/blog/?p=28890
110 ibid

"Many Iraqi tank crews had turned their engines off to let their vehicles cool down in the night air, which confounded our thermal optics and led to a 360 degree battle as we passed tanks we thought had been defeated by the 2nd ACR. The battle lasted until sun up.

"The last shot was fired by COB6 when he launched a TOW missile into a T55 Iraqi tank. In the end, the U.S. 1st infantry Division had destroyed the 18th Mechanized Brigade and 37th Armored Brigade of the Tawakalna Division.

"The Iraqis stood their ground at Norfolk, which gave other Iraqi units time to escape from Kuwait, but at a terrible cost to the Iraqi army, which lost hundreds of tanks and thousands of soldiers in the twelve-hour engagement."[111]

It is really interesting to read other blogs about a TC (Tank Commander) as he operates in the dark.[112] I asked Paul Hook to clarify the tanker's language and he offered the following:

"You are correct that TC stands for tank commander. TC buttoned up refers to when the hatch is fully closed. This mode is used when artillery or chemical threats are present or impending.

"TC protected refers to when the hatch is in a partially open position, with the hatch cover protecting the tank commander from overhead airburst artillery, provides better visibility than fully buttoned, while still offering better protection for the tank commander than 'Open' status.

---

111 ibid
112 http://www.tanksim.com/topic14.htm

"TC un-buttoned (open) refers to when the hatch is open. This mode provides the tank commander with maximum visibility, but it is susceptible to sniper fire, grenades, and shrapnel. This mode is seldom used during actual combat.

"Units wear MOPP (Mission Oriented Protective Posture) gear regardless of whether the tank is buttoned or not. The standard operating procedures for individual units may require MOPP to be worn at a certain level depending on whether the tank is buttoned, protected, or un-buttoned."[113]

BATTLE FOR JALIBAH SOUTHEAST AIRFIELD:

About 6:00 AM, on February 27, 1991, "Satellite and aircraft reconnaissance indicated the presence of twenty enemy tanks and more than one thousand dug-in Iraqi soldiers at an airfield eighty miles east of Basra. At 6 a.m. on the morning of 27 February, following an intensive artillery barrage, about two hundred vehicles of the 1st Brigade, under the command of General Paul J. Kern, charged into the airfield and secured it after four hours of fighting.

"According to 2nd Lieutenant Neal Creighton, Iraqi soldiers 'tried to hide in shallow bunkers and some of them tried to surrender. Most of the soldiers who moved were quickly cut down under a swath of machine gun fire. The burning helicopters, jets, and dead soldiers seemed almost unreal—my soldiers were alive. It was the happiest moment of my life.' Major David S. Pierson, who served as a task-force intelligence captain in the 1st Brigade, said he eventually felt 'guilty that we had slaughtered them so;

---

113 Paul Hook, personal correspondence.

guilty that we had performed so well and they so poorly; guilty that we were running up the score. They were like children fleeing before us—unorganized, scared, wishing it all would end. We continued to pour it on."

"Only one U.S. soldier was wounded by enemy fire during this battle. In the confusion, however, three U.S. M2 Bradley infantry fighting vehicles of C Company, 3rd Battalion, and 15th Infantry Regiment were accidentally hit with depleted uranium rounds fired by the tanks of C Company, 3rd Battalion, and 69th Armor Regiment. This friendly fire incident resulted in the ten additional American casualties: two deaths and eight injuries."[114]

---

114 http://en.wikipedia.org/wiki/Battle_for_Jalibah_Airfield

CHAPTER 7
FEBRUARY 27, 1991–FEBRUARY 28, 1991. The Last B-52s Over Baghdad in Gulf War I

For He shall give His angels charge over thee,
to keep thee in all thy ways —**Psalms 91:11**

*A*s I'm writing this, it seems incongruous to write some of the subtitle chapter quotations with semi profanity and others with sanctimony. My chaplains would understand. *However, as you will see, the above Bible quotation is appropriate for this part of the story.*

To learn more about the B52, one of the most durable heavy bombers in U.S. history, I researched the Internet to some extent, but I harvested more of the pertinent information I desired from interviews and conversations with two former crewmembers: my oldest son, Bill, a former B52 pilot; and one of his former crewmates and current brother-in-law, Navigator Mike Tichenor. Still on active duty, Mike is a regular officer in the USAF. He is currently Chief of Air Operations at Barksdale AFB, Louisiana, and I'll start with his interview from June 8, 2012.

"Col. Michael A. Tichenor is the Commander of the 608th

Air Operations Center, 8th Air Force at Barksdale AFB, in Louisiana, where he is responsible for the operational level strategy, the planning, and the command and control of global airpower for the 8th Air Force assets from the 2nd Bomb Wing at Barksdale AFB in Louisiana, the 5th Bomb Wing at Minot AFB in North Dakota, and the 509th Bomb Wing at Whiteman AFB in Missouri.

COLONEL MICHAEL A. TICHENOR

"As a command navigator, the colonel has more than three thousand hours in both the B-52G/H and B-1. Colonel Tichenor amassed one hundred combat hours during Operation Allied Force."[115]

Colonel Mike Tichenor Interview:

WFH   "Col. Tichenor, you graduated from The University of Minnesota. When was that?"

MT   "1987. June 1987."

WFH   "Then you went directly into the Air Force?"

---

115 http://www.8af.af.mil/library/biographies/bio.asp?id=14269

MT   "Actually I had to wait about eleven months, and I didn't get to the Air Force until May '88."

WFH   "Yes, I think that was the same thing that happened to Bill. So, where did you go for your first training as a navigator?"

MT   "Mather AFB up in Sacramento[116] I got there in November of '88 for Navigator training."

WFH   "When Desert Shield was heating up, were you still in California?"

MT   "No. By that time I had made it through Navigator School and B-52 Training and got to KI Sawyer AFB just before Desert Shield had heated up. I got to KI Sawyer in April of 1990."

WFH   "You knew Bill then, but you were not on his crew?"

MT   "That's right. I was not on his crew then."

WFH   "Tell me about where you sit in a B-52. Where does the navigator sit?"

MT   "The navigator sits behind the pilots but on a second level. We call it 'downstairs.'"

WFH   "Are you the ones that eject down?"

MT   "Right. The Navigator and the Radar Navigator."

WFH   "So, how many crewmen are on a B-52?"

MT   "Right now it's five. It used to be six. Back in those days there was still a Gunner on board, and he sat up front with everybody else. He actually sat backwards. But after Desert Storm they decided that the gunnery

---

116 Mather is now closed

	system was (A) too hard to maintain and (B) really not that effective in keeping fighters away."
WFH	"Okay. The B-52—the Buff, that's what they call it?"
MT	"Uh-huh."
WFH	(I laugh because I know that B.U.F.F. stands for Big Ugly Fat F-----er) "Ok. Tell me about your equipment. I'm not asking for classified stuff. Did you have GPS?"
MT	"That was an interesting time. GPS was brand new. The constellation had just been finished—all twenty-seven satellites that it takes to establish the GPS constellation. So, not all B-52's were outfitted with GPS. In fact, the B-52's that we had at KI Sawyer, which were primarily nuclear B-52's, didn't have GPS. *The G models, that was back* in the days when we had ten or eleven B-52 bases and two hundred some-odd B-52's, about half were G models and half were H Models. The G models that were slightly older were not committed to the nuclear mission and they were actually fitted with GPS. And those were the ones that were flying in Desert Storm primarily. So, those of us who were flying in the H models, if we were going to fly in Desert Storm, had to go get trained in how to use the GPS; plus, the gunnery system was a little bit different, so we had to learn that as well. The Gunners had to go through extensive conversion training, as we called it, out in California."
WFH	"Didn't you fly some missions from Sawyer in the States?"
MT	"No. The guys who flew missions out of the States—and not necessarily back—flew out of Wurtsmith Air Force

Base in Michigan (Wurtsmith was closed in 1993), performed night bombing runs, and then landed in the theater. And the guys out of Barksdale, Louisiana— they had been working on what was at that point a highly classified mission where they took old nuclear air-launch cruise missiles and converted them into conventional missiles so they would have the capability to stand away from the target over five hundred miles and launch these things with decent precision and strike targets. And that was called the conventional air launch cruise missile, called the CALCUM. The guys from Barksdale can't remember how many planes— two or four, fully loaded with about twenty of those things each—flew several missions, night ones as well, and launched a bunch of those things to take out air defense targets."

WFH   "You know I was surprised. I flew one medevac mission into Jeddah of all places, and Jeddah had a B-52 base. Not many people knew about that."

MT   "Uh-huh."

WFH   "I took out my camera to take a picture, and I felt a hand on my shoulder. A voice said, 'Colonel, you'd better put that away.' I thought I was in trouble."

MT   "I think Jeddah was where a lot of the guys from Wurtsmith landed after they had done their mission."

WFH   "Okay. So were you still at Sawyer when all that was going on?"

MT   "Yes, I still remember when CNN was talking all about the Gulf War and the bombings and most of the B-52's were still at Sawyer on restricted alert, but pulling nuclear alerts at that time. Six of the B-52's were on nuclear alert at any one time at Sawyer, and we were restricted to the building and couldn't go anywhere because you just had to keep your nuclear forces close at hand at that point when that kind of a thing was going on."

WFH   "How many squadrons of B-52's did they have on hand at Sawyer?"

MT   "Just one, but it was very big. It was a twenty-four-crew squadron."

WFH   "So, when Bill was deployed not all the crews went?"

MT   "No, I think he went with only two crews. He and one other crew went and then there were some follow-on crews, which I was a part of. The reason they were asking for more crews was that the guys who were flying were flying so often that they were running out of crew-flight times. You can only fly so many hours in a month. These guys were bumping up against that, and they needed to sit down."

WFH   "Well, you know, the only intelligence we had was CNN."

MT   "Un-huh, which was pretty good!"

WFH   "Which wasn't bad, but you know, we didn't get direct briefings. I used to go out to Al Dhafra and sit in Operations and watch those sorties go and listen to their chatter. They said they dropped more ordnance in those forty-three days than had been dropped in Europe throughout all of WWII."

MT   "Yup."

WFH   "Unbelievable!"

MT   "It is unbelievable."

WFH   "But I watched them go and I believe it! It was really something. Now do you remember who your commander was—your Squadron Commander?"

MT   "Yeah, oh what's his name?"

WFH   "That's ok I can probably look it up."

MT   "No, no it will come to me. I remember my company commander and some of the others."

WFH   "That's ok. I've got pictures and I can't tag names on some of the guys and gals. But then, it's twenty some years later. What was your unit designation?"

MT   "We were the 644th Bomb Squadron of the 410th Bombardment Wing out of KI Sawyer."

WFH   "Tell me about the most dramatic, memorable, or exciting moment while you were there."

MT   "It was actually post Desert Storm, but it would have been the most interesting. And that was at KI when it was a small part of Operation Southern Watch, when there was a no-fly zone over Southern Iraq and also over Iraq's northern border. Basically, the purpose was to not allow Iraqi aircraft to fly near their southern or northern borders. But anyway, we did a month-long deployment and took two B-52's and two tankers to Guam, Australia, Thailand, and Diego Garcia, which included flying training missions from Diego Garcia up near Iraq just like they did in Desert Storm. We flew missions out of Diego Garcia up to the Gulf and back just to let them know we were there as kind of a deterrent—that there were still B-52's in the area and you guys pay attention because we can bring them up any time we want. That was kind of fun, showing the flag in Australia and Guam and Thailand as well. Guam is also a large bomber staging base."

WFH   "Tell me more about the B-52 itself. You said there was a crew of five?"

MT   "There were six at that time; it's down to five now."

WFH   "Okay. So there were you, the pilot, and co-pilot. Who were the other three?"

MT   "There were actually three with a navigator designation. The two with the more traditional navigator designations were the Navigator and the Radar Navigator. This came about because originally it took one guy to see to it that the system, i.e. the Navigation System, was running properly and that the plane knew where it was. So that was the Radar Navigator and he was like the senior guy. Then there was the Navigator, who was typically a young Captain or Lieutenant, and he operated those systems that were being monitored by this other guy (the senior Radar Navigator). Then he directed the plane where to go and be on time, and he made sure that the weapon systems were operating properly and were ready to fire."

WFH   "And he would act as the bombardier then?"

MT   "That was what the Radar Navigator was. He would traditionally be the bombardier from the old days. So really, if you took a B-17 (A WWII heavy bomber), which had a bombardier and a navigator, the bombardier just became the Radar Navigator because you now have a radar system that keeps everything up to speed, and since he's the senior guy he is responsible for where the bombs go."

WFH "And you have an anti-missile defense system?"

MT "Yes, and that was the third guy. The third navigator-designated guy was called the electronic warfare operator (EWO), and he operated a pretty effective system—an intensive manual system. It could detect both air defenses and missile launches and early warning radar, and it could do some jamming against them. He was a pretty busy man during the five to ten minutes of combat, and he did nothing during the rest of the sortie."

Author's note: The 6th Crewman in a B-52 in Desert Storm was the Gunner. He sat up front with the other crew, but facing backwards as previously stated by Colonel Tichenor.

The 1991 B-52 crew in summary:

- Pilot
- Co-Pilot
- Radar Navigator (Bombardier)
- Navigator
- EWO the electronic warfare officer
- Gunner

WFH "Well thank you very much. That's all very interesting."

MT "You're welcome."

In an article published in *Stars and Stripes*[117] on January 6, 1991, Melissa Healy of the Los Angeles Times addressed the U.S.'s recycled B-52 bombing strategy. Referring to the ancient bomber as venerable and the Air Force's plans to use carpet bombing as being even older, Healy indicated that the proposed strategy for Desert Shield, if it were to become Desert Storm, was if anything "low tech."

Healy's description indicated that our more modern aircraft would eliminate enemy fighters and air defenses. Then the slow, lumbering bombers, whose crews were even younger than their aircraft, would proceed to destroy Iraqi troops and fortifications. She also noted correctly that U.S. strategists believed that after days of steady bombardment the enemy would be so traumatized that there would not be much resistance in a ground fight.

At the time she wrote it, Healy did not know how correctly the planners had predicted the results. The only difference was that although the B-52's were undoubtedly effective, just as much credit should be given the around-the-clock fighter-bomber sorties who were attacking Iraq out of bases like Al Dhafra, Navy aircraft carriers, and other Allied resources—not to mention the AWACS[118] controlling the skies.

Healy noted that Pentagon officials and planners had conceded that there was controversy over the effectiveness of carpet-bombing, also called strategic bombing. Ground commanders in particular were said to have been concerned that the process

117 *Stars and Stripes*. Vol. 49, No. 265. Sunday, January 6, 1991 (p. 1)
118 Airborne Warning and Control Systems

would scatter thousands of land mines that Iraq had lain, thus creating more hazards for advancing troops and armor.

She also noted that the B-52 force had shrunk to no more than forty bombers, but someone had given her an obviously false figure when the later unclassified number related by Colonel Tichenor was over two hundred, twenty-four of which were at K.I. Sawyer AFB.

In actuality, the B-52 strategy was much more strategic than carpet-bombing, and in my opinion the terms should not be used as synonyms. From what I've learned, all of the B-52 targets were strategic, such as the tank factories that Bill's flight attacked. Although admittedly their bombs were not guided or smart, the collateral damage was still much lower than it would have been with a carpet strategy.

Bill Hook gives the B-52 Commander's view: "Carpet bombing does not equal strategic bombing. Strategic bombing targets assets to take away the enemy's ability to wage war. The missions of the Cold War era, in case it should become "hot" were to destroy the USSR's war fighting capability.

"In that sense you could argue that carpet bombing was a form of strategic bombing, since it took away Iraq's ability to wage war against the Coalition. Tactical bombing would target assets to win a battle. Somewhere in between would be the approach of asset allocation and modalities selection to win a campaign or a theater which would be at an operational level of planning. That is where I would put or categorize carpet bombing.

"Another way of thinking is simply that is exactly what the B-52 did, i.e. carpet-bomb. That is because it laid down so many weapons that it exceeded any other platform. Only the B-52 at the time, and now the B-1 and B-2 can lay down a carpet of destruction."[119]

The other side of the coin is illustrated by one of Healy's other military source experts, who was quoted as saying that we knew exactly where the Iraqi entrenchments were and we could eliminate them in a couple of days. Although Healy suggested in her article that this strategy would involve the B-52's, in actuality they were mostly destroyed by allied fighter-bombers using smart bombs, as televised by CNN and other TV news programs. However, it's possible that some of these targets could have been attacked by B-52's using the CALCUMs (Conventional Air Launched Cruise Missiles) as described by Col. Tichenor.

The bottom line is that Allied air power was extremely effective. It kept U.S. and Coalition casualties to a minimum and shortened what could have been a much longer war.

Next, I will present recollections of Captain Bill Hook's mission over Baghdad. Bill is my first-born son, born at the U.S. Naval Hospital, Pensacola, Florida on August 14, 1961, while I was an intern serving on the OB service. I was on a gurney that was being wheeled past the room where his mother was in labor, desperately holding a baby's head away from a prolapsed umbilical cord on another patient and trying to prevent a fetal strangulation on the way to the operating room. We did get a good baby out of the C-section thanks to a bold surgeon who made a fast but slightly deep incision not only through the patient's abdominal wall and gestational uterus

---

119 Bill Hook personal correspondence 12-1-2012.

but also through the back of my gloved hand. Bill's mother Margo and I got a good baby too, even though it had been a high forceps delivery with the fetus in distress. It was a memorable day twice over.

Bill's curriculum vitae includes two years at the Air Force Academy, a voluntary transfer to Stanford with an undergraduate two-major degree in Mechanical Engineering and Biological Science (Stanford class of 1985), an ROTC commission from San Jose State, ten years as an Air Force pilot, an MD degree from the University of Michigan, service as Chief Resident of Family Practice, a return to active duty as a Medical Officer USAF, and eventually finished the military portion of his career as the Chief of Medical Staff, Ramstein Air Force Base, Germany.

Ramstein is just down the hill, a short six kilometers away from Landstuhl Regional Medical Center. LRMC is the large Army facility that takes in most of our combat casualties from all branches of service serving the Middle East. Bill practiced at Ramstein, LRMC and Sembach AFB fifteen minutes East of Ramstein before becoming the Medical Chief of Staff at Ramstein.

He is the recipient of numerous decorations. Besides his service in Desert Storm, Col. Hook has served in Afghanistan, and has one tour in Iraq and one in North Africa. He is certified by the American Board of Family Practice.

Top Photo: Col. William C. Hook, MC USAF Medical
Chief of Staff, Ramstein AFB, Landstuhl, Germany, June 2012.

Bottom Photo: 2nd.LT Bill Hook circa 1986-87 standing by his T38 Talon jet trainer.

DESERT STORM'S LAST BOMBING MISSION OVER BAGHDAD: FEBRUARY 27–28, 1991

Bill's Tale: the following recall is an excerpt from Bill's USAF retirement ceremony speech as the Chief of Staff of Ramstein Medical Services given on June 11, 2012. The recording was started as Bill was talking about the day leading up to his last combat mission in Desert Storm. WCH is Capt. (now Col.) William Charles Hook—call sign Hooker—Commander of B-52 # 6 in a flight of six on the very last bombing raid on Baghdad during Gulf War I, from Wednesday February 27–Thursday February 28, 1991.

> WCH: (discussing the heavy bombing schedules out of Diego Garcia): "So, I get added in, my crew gets added in and scheduled to fly that Wednesday, but that day with the rapid advance of our ground troops all of our targets were now behind the advancing troops and in friendly territory. So, all day long the mission board showed: 'cancel, cancel, cancel, cancel.' But ours was a nighttime interdiction mission. When we finally flew it, it was to take out targets south of Baghdad, which were tank factories. The combat mission was 15.4 hours (from Diego Garcia and back) and actually it wasn't until about two years after I got back that I told Debbie that we had volunteered for that mission. She said loudly, 'You what?' I had kept that kind of quiet (The audience laughs).
>
> "The mission was a six-bomber flight, and I was the new kid on the block in this particular flight, so that's why we were the number six bomber—the last one in and out. We

got briefed about 1:00 in the afternoon and took off about 5:00. We struck Baghdad between 0200 and 0300 and flew in at different angles to the target, and two ships flew around and came in from different directions at different times, to assure a better chance at its destruction.

Author's note: the distance from Diego Garcia to Baghdad is just over 2,900 nautical miles and the cruising speed of a B-52 is about 442Kts (525mph); so, an uneventful round trip flight without air refueling, which is not possible due to the limited range of a B-52, would be just over thirteen hours. The total mission time for this sortie was 15.4 hours. I initially thought the excess mission time involved was partly due to bombing tactics, which required the six plane flight to approach the targets from different angles, altitudes, times, and directions, but also due to the time spent with air-to-air refueling.

My engineer, pilot, physician son straightened me out:

"In summary we were essentially seven or so hours to the Saudi-Iraqi border with two refuelings, about an hour and a half in country (Iraq) and another seven hours or so back. The time was a little shorter going back because we needed only one more refueling, being lighter and therefore more fuel efficient.

"The six ship takeoff formation actually broke up into flights of four and two aircraft each very early in the mission. Each flight then had its own set of refueling tracks and tankers.

"The B-52 G was a "water wagon", which meant it had water injected engines that provided a greater temperature differential between combustion and exhaust and therefore provided a greater thrust to get the 488,000 pound bird off the ground. All of the fully loaded takeoffs from hot and humid Diego Garcia were water augmented and that meant taking on more fuel during aerial refueling because the 10,000 pounds of water weight used for takeoff meant there was 10,000 pounds less fuel in the tanks.

"Interestingly, once airborne, the B-52G could take on much more gas than what they took off with, and bring the weight up to 540,000 pounds or so. (The newer H Model B-52s have more powerful Pratt & Whitney turbofan engines and don't use water injection)."[120]

So now I know that the bombing tactics did not affect the mission time very much, but the air-to-air refueling certainly did.

In addition, the number six bomber that was flown by Capt. Bill Hook experienced problems with air-to-air refueling after the ground-to-air missile attack in which they experienced a significant compression shock wave after narrowly averting an enemy missile. There are also three time zones between Diego Garcia and Baghdad, the targets being further west.

Bill continued his father's education: "To clarify; the problems on the third and last refueling had nothing to do with the transit time other than being on a refueling track. I later learned that the problem was with the electrical contact that sent a signal back to the tanker that the boom was engaged to allow its system to pump. It was either dirty or damaged from two earlier refuelings or it was just plain time to replace the part"[121]

---

120 Bill Hook, personal correspondence, Dec.1, 2012
121 Ibid.

WCH (continues his retirement speech excerpt): "I knew what time the bombs were going to be dropped and therefore I knew what times some Iraqi's would die. I prayed for my co-pilot, the crew, and myself. I prayed for the Iraqi mothers whose sons were going to die. It was then, as the ships went across the target that my training kicked in and I became a sort of automaton, if you will. After the first four ships went across the targets, there were still shock waves and ripples from the bomb explosions and the anti-aircraft missiles. I'm the tail-end Charlie, and from the ground reaction my co-pilot and the navigators could tell that the Iraqis were pretty upset. I was focused on flying and lining up the flight direction indicator thereby putting the plane where the Radar Navigator wanted it to go so he could release the bombs. It was like flying on the fourth of July—not quite like the movie *The Memphis Belle*, but close. We could see the unguided missiles coming up. The EWO (Electronic Warfare Officer) confirmed that one unguided SA 6 (a Russian made surface to air missile) that had a homing signal but was not locked on to us[122] blew up just aft of us releasing a horrendous compression wave forward, but there was not enough shrapnel to take out our tail, which had happened to some of my colleagues who had come back with damaged planes. It didn't do that, but

---

122 The Iraqi Surface-to-Air Missile crews had learned early on not to use their lock-on radar because it made them vulnerable to destruction from our anti-missile defense systems, or fighter escorts in the area.

the compression wave released enough energy that we entered a stall and my co-pilot yelled, 'We lost all eight. We lost all eight (engines)!'

AUTHOR'S NOTE: I initially thought the aft exploding SAM caused a compression wave that forced the B-52's tail down resulting in a nose up stall of the wings. My engineer son straightened me out again:

"The compression stall was across the engine blades, not the wings, and was due to the brief shockwave flow of air meeting the rearward thrust. The rpms and eprs (engine propulsion ratios) of all eight engines dropped suddenly and just as quickly resumed the level they were supposed to be just as Joe Hyde (the co-pilot) finished his exclamation."[123]

WCH (continued): "As we recovered from the stall, we could see that the ship was intact and all eight engines were working. Shortly after that, we released our bombs. Then there was just a long silence while we waited for the explosions. Then there was another missile warning from the EWO and another explosion. I asked the EWO if we got hit. I got a negative report and found that we were still airworthy. Then the expressions escaped, and I'm not saying from whom: 'Let's get the colorful bleep out of here!' (The audience laughs).

"Then, on the way back we had some more excitement. On the (air-to-air) refueling procedure, the gas connection kept coming loose and we had to do a manual override, which is never done and is verboten. If that hadn't

---

worked, the navigator was already plotting a course to get us to the coast before we ran out of gas. It did work, however, and once we were back I called Debbie on one of those many dollars-a-minute wireless calls and told her that we had flown a mission— that it was kind of an eye-opener but that I felt that we had an angel underneath us and that everything was ok and we were untouched.

"Unbeknownst to me, my co-pilot's mom is back in Texas, and she had gone to her priest requesting prayers for her son who was flying in Iraq. The priest asked her, 'What does he fly?' When she answered 'a B-52' the priest said, 'Really? I had this dream last night. There were B- 52s flying over a target and there was an angel under the last one over the target'. So I became a good Catholic boy and believed that. That's kind of the way I practice medicine too: prayers when appropriate and faith in the Almighty."

I then followed up Bill's tale with an interview that I recorded on the way to the Frankfurt International Airport on June 12, 2012."

WFH   "So, at what time did you get back from that mission?"

WCH   "It was daylight in Diego Garcia, around 8:00 or 9:00 in the morning, when we landed, and about noon by the time we got debriefed and went to bed. I probably didn't talk to Debbie until the next day, after I slept, but it's possible I called her that afternoon."

WFH   "So how did you talk to Debbie?"

WCH   "There is a British communications company named Cable and Wireless, known by some of my colleagues as 'Cable and Heartless 'because the cost at that time in 1991 was a couple of dollars a minute. You put your money in first and then watch the time tick down as you talk. That's when I told her about our experiences that night. I told her that we had monitored on the radio a rescue mission of a couple of guys who hadn't been over here for very long and who were shot down and I did say that we had some stuff—missiles and AAA-Anti-Aircraft Artillery—coming up but not to worry because we had an angel underneath us to keep us out of harm's way. It actually was about a week later that my co-pilot told me about his mother and the priest."

WFH   "And who was this fellow that had the dream?"

WCH   "An Episcopal Priest in Texas. There was actually a book or a chapter in a book about it. I'll have to get back to you on this because I don't have the name."

Author's note: The book is titled *To See His Goodness.*, by Marianne Gerdes Smith., Morris Publishing: Kerney, NE. Bill's co-pilot was Joe Glenn Hyde III, whose father, Joe G. Hyde Jr., was the much-publicized U2 pilot lost over Cuba in 1963 just before JFK's assassination. Marianne Smith is Joe's mother.

WFH   "Ok. You said that when you got to the target the bombers crossed the target from angles. They crossed at right angles, huh?"

WCH   "At angles—not necessarily *right* angles."

WFH   "What's the purpose of that—just to stay out of each other's way or what?"

WCH   "No. Actually, it's a very common technique. If you need to take out an infrastructure, let's say the road we're driving on right now, you don't travel directly along the road and drop all your bombs there. You come across it at an angle to be sure you take out a section. If you were directly over it a factor like wind or a minor change of direction might cause you to miss entirely. That was then. Maybe now there's something entirely different, like laser guidance, GPS control or whatever. But the common technique from WWI on was to come at a target at an acute angle so that one or more of your bombs in the stick would be on target—like a railroad depot with lots of tracks. You don't go down a line parallel to the tracks because you might miss or just take out one or two lines. If you go across at an angle you will likely take out parts of many tracks."

Author's note: Laser-guided bombs—or so-called smart bombs—were commonly used in Gulf War One, but not by the B-52's, which were usually on higher altitude missions with no available laser in range to paint the target. However, Bill was right that something was new. An on-line article by Mike Hanlon of *Gizmag* best describes the new technology.[124] The new bombs are deadly accurate. Guided by GPS technology, they are actually labeled as GBUs, which stands for Guided Bomb Units.

In this article, Hanlon describes the newest weapon. The GBU-57 A/B, as the ultimate MOP (Massive Ordnance Penetrator) which is specifically designed to penetrate and destroy hardened concrete bunkers, which shield important targets like command and control facilities or house weapons of mass destruction. He also notes that

124 http://www.gizmag.com/massive-ordnance-penetrator-mop-gbu-57ab/20538/

the GBU acronym can be found on nearly everything that drops from a USAF plane in this modern era, but this latest bomb weighs thirty thousand pounds, and when dropped from significant altitude, it can penetrate up to two hundred feet of hardened concrete before it explodes. (Perhaps Iran's Ahmadinejad should take notice. We don't even use weapons anymore that cannot be dropped precisely where we want them to go.)

We then talked about Bill's recent 2012 deployment to North Africa. I was aware of his location while he was there. Suffice it to say, there are some interesting diseases in North Africa, which we discussed. Bill said he is interested in someday possibly returning as a medical missionary to the village where he lived during his tour. For now he is scheduled to retire from active duty in the fall of 2012, and is planning to join a group family practice in Escanaba, Michigan.

Above: B-52, H model. The H models are expected to remain in service until 2040. U.S. Air Force photo.

I was able to track down the book written by Joe Glenn Hyde's mother,[125] and in the epilogue Mrs. Smith describes her encounter with the priest who was the rector of her parish. His name was Ellis Brust and he was in charge of St. Paul's Episcopal Church in Katy, Texas, which is a suburb of Houston. Joe's widowed mother, Marianne, joined the Episcopal Church after marrying Horace Smith.

Joe's first assignment as a co-pilot on a B-52 crew was in Guam, but after his marriage he was assigned to K.I. Sawyer AFB in Marquette, Michigan, where he became Bill's co-pilot.

Marianne Smith's description varied slightly from the story told to Bill. The Priest's dream was not a dream, nor did it occur at night. It was a vision that apparently occurred to the clergyman during an intense public prayer in church as Mrs. Smith stopped the Priest while he was on his way to the vestry to get ready for a service.

When she heard about the B-52 that had gone down on its way back to Diego Garcia, Marianne had been as worried as I had been. Thus she stopped Reverend Brust and told him how worried she was. When Brust heard of her concern he laid both of his hands on her shoulders and started an intense and very public prayer for Joe Glenn's[126] safety in front of the parishioners, who were waiting for the services to start. He then said that he had seen an angel holding up a B-52. Joe's mother suggested in

---

125 *To See His Goodness.* Marianne Gerdes Smith. Morris Publishing: Kerney, NE. 1999 (p. 199)

126 Joe's mother always called him by his middle name, Glenn.

the book that it must have been a very large angel to hold up a B-52.

My own take on the priest's comment on seeing an angel holding up the B-52 is that it was likely a comment of re-assurance for Mrs. Smith, a statement of faith. Does that mean I discounted a possible actual vision? Absolutely not. Whatever the realty was, I have no desire to create controversy and unwanted publicity by investigating and have not tried to contact Reverend Brust. Don't you find it interesting though that two individuals, thousands of miles apart used the same words to describe a possible Devine Intervention as the answer to different prayers? I do and would like to believe that there are indeed such things as Guardian Angels. With that kind of faith the occurrence of an actual vision by a clergyman becomes irrelevant.

Another interesting fact that came out of Smith's book was that she did not think too much about the angel at the time because she had heard Bush's speech that the war was over before she knew about Bill, Joe, their crew's mission, and the near miss by the surface-to-air missile, which was why she hadn't given Reverend Brust's statement about the angel very much attention at first.

When she did communicate with her son, and he told her that he had also heard Bush's speech in the cockpit while returning to Diego Garcia,[127] she did tell Joe Glenn about the priest, the prayer, and the vision. In addition, she stated in her book that

---

127 Bill confirmed that they listened to a BBC broadcast of President Bush's speech on the way back to Diego Garcia.

Bill's mother, my ex-wife Margo Boothe Turkington, had also had a similar vision.

Now, I know that Margo was a somewhat skeptical Christian who was not prone to believing in such things, and I have no idea how Mrs. Smith heard about Margo's experience or even if she had ever communicated with Margo. Bill denies any knowledge of his mother having a vision, but he did say that he was aware that Margo and my middle son, Chris, had had a session with a Ouija board in which an entity claiming to be an angel communicated with them after interrupting the session and replacing another entity who was, according to the angel, evil. This session apparently was held shortly after the war was over and when both Chris and Margo were aware of Bill's mission and the priest's prayer. Thus they queried the second entity about the mission and asked if he was the angel involved. The answer returned was: "No, that was Raphael. God said it was important."

Bill's take on Margo's and Chris's experience: "Who are we to limit what God can and cannot do? That answer is easy we can't. After all He takes bad situations and brings good out of them on a regular, even routine, basis." Bill was referring to the Roman Catholic position that Ouija boards or other divining devices are mostly denied as coming from God.

I think it's more likely that Margo's experience with the Ouija board somehow got translated to "a vision" in Mrs. Smith's book, than an actual vision occurred, but who knows? Perhaps it is true. Chris died in 1995 and Margo died in 1999.

I guess the Lord does indeed work in mysterious ways.

One more fascinating coincidence is Bill's comment to his crew while they were enroute back to Diego Garcia and after they had heard President Bush's remarks that the war was over. Here is his quote:

"I recall that in the cockpit we heard a BBC broadcast on the high frequency radio. The EWO was monitoring it and then shared with the crew what was coming across. I don't recall if we heard an excerpt of President Bush's statements or simply a report of them. But I do recall quite clearly that I said over the intercom, 'Well boys, it looks like we won it since we were the last ones out, but the job's not over. We're going to have to come back within ten years to finish the job.'"

Now check my remarks in Chapter 9, under the first manuscript bullet which describes a conversation which occurred over twenty years ago. Bill has never seen them and I never told him about the Iraqi physician. (see page 152).

Bill had a few more asides on the mission:

"After we successfully got our gas for the trip back to Diego Garcia, we had a chance to relax before assuming the business of approach and landing. The comment I made of how we won it led to a cacophony of joking comments on how humble little crew R-54 from KI Sawyer won Desert Storm. But Radar Navigator Fred Degasperin made one sobering joke that you don't really win a war until you are drinking beer on the steps of the enemy's city hall, then added something along the lines of he does not foresee us having a beer in Baghdad and he couldn't even have a beer right now for that matter. Funny Guy, Fred."[128]

---

128 Bill Hook , personal correspondence 12.2, 2012

The number six B-52 crew on the last bombing mission over Baghdad:

Pilot:	Captain William Charles Hook
Co-Pilot:	Captain Joseph Glenn Hyde III
Radar Navigator	Captain Fred Degasperin
Navigator	Captain Eric Nier
EWO	Captain Scott Barbu
Gunner	Staff Sergeant Travis Hammond[129]

---

129 Sergeant Hammond was killed after the war trying to stop a robbery in a convenience store.

CHAPTER 8
FEBRUARY 28, 1991–MARCH 10, 1991. EPWs: the Enemy Prisoners of War

A prisoner of war is a man who tries to kill you and fails, and then asks you not to kill him. —**Winston Churchill**

*T*hursday, February 28: "I received a call today from the 202nd and had an hour to get six doctors and ten medics ready to ship to the POW camp that is run by the 403rd MPs. I dispatched Major George S. Hsu—pronounced 'Shoe'—a family practitioner from Elgin, North Dakota; his wife SSG Kathy Hsu, a 91 Charlie; and surgeons Tad Gilmore, Pokey Cleek, Virgil Hayden, Roger Allen, and John Wade, along with nine other medics. They will be attached to the 403rd MPs for EPW care near the (Kuwaiti) border. (I am) to expect more similar orders since counting previous transfers 1/3 of my doctors are now gone. There was a cease-fire today as reported by CNN. General Schwarzkopf was magnificent last night."

Surgeons Gilmore, Cleek, and Wade were FNGs—Faultless New Guys. Norris E. (Pokey) Cleek was a talented general surgeon who was from the wine country of northern California if my memory serves me correctly. Minot, North Dakota was Roger Allen's hometown. He was in the 311th before we were activated, and he was a practicing pediatrician. We moved him to an ENT slot before mobilization.

I knew George Hsu from the Bismarck section of the 311th and we worked together occasionally when I was the consulting radiologist at the Elgin Hospital. I knew George was a combat veteran in Viet Nam, where his MOSQ made him a qualified explosive ordnance disposal specialist. Considering all the threats that I was aware of from the intelligence folks at the American Embassy, I was glad to have his skills available, even though we never needed them.

The new orders, which potentially had more personnel changes, convinced me that we would not see any additional battle casualties, and I was correct. On reviewing the statistics of the three Evac hospitals in the Southern Gulf, we treated just over fifty military patients who were evacuated to CONUS (Continental United States) and hundreds of military personnel from all branches of service who were either hospitalized or treated and returned to duty. A number of surgeries were performed, including the usual appendectomies, hernia repairs, and arthroscopies that we would see as civilians, as well as non-combat injuries, accidents, and trauma. We did handle a few combat casualties, the most serious of which, as I recall, was a penetrating chest wound. No combat-related deaths occurred on our watch, but we came close to having one death as our consulting surgeons heroically saved a civilian OB-GYN patient with a life threatening hemorrhage. That particular case is noteworthy because of the reluctance of the Arabs to allow a male physician to treat one of their women.

As Dr. Hayden tells the story: "Once an occasion arose when Major Cleek (Pokey) helped me save the life of one of the locals' wife. She had had a C-section and encountered unbelievable bleeding. I quickly put on a gown and gloves. I had to reach into the abdomen to grasp the bleeders. Major Cleek was summoned to assist me. Once he joined me, we proceeded to repair the uterine artery that had been lacerated in three places. After the repairs were completed and the patient stabilized, she was sent to the ICU. She was better the next day, but she required eight to ten units of blood. We could not follow this case because we were sent up to assist with the EPWs."[130]

The EPW Mission, Dr. Gilmore's After Action Report (edited): February 28, 1991–March 10, 1991

"Our mission began by being transported from Al Dhafra by C-130 to Dhahran on 28 February 1991. Contact with 173rd Med group was made and the next a.m. we were transported to the site of the 300th Field Hospital approximately 40 km north of Al Shara. That evening we made contact with Col. Novak, Commander of the 403rd MP (Military Police) Camp and Maj. Longacre, the camp medical officer. We encountered some initial problems with communicating and interpreting our tasking orders among the 300th Field Hospital, the 403rd MP Camp, and ourselves. These were dealt with and resolved, which resulted in our moving to the 403rd MP Camp early the next a.m. and starting our job with one team

---

130 Jacobsen. *A Story of the 311*th (p. 51)

of two physicians and three medics going to the in-processing area of the EPW camp and a second team consisting of one physician and two medics going to the EPW enclosure to provide sick call because none had been provided for several days. In addition, one medic was assigned to drive an ambulance."

"Prior to our arrival, approximately five hundred EPWs per day were being in-processed each twenty-four-hour period. There were between two thousand and three thousand EPWs that were unprocessed in holding, and more were being added in large numbers several times a day. In our first twenty-four hours, 760 EPWs were in-processed. In the next two days, personnel from the 300th Field Hospital gradually assumed medical coverage of the EPW enclosures, and personnel from the 403rd MP medical team were provided to drive the ambulance, thus freeing our entire group to do our task assignment.

"On Sunday, March 3, we in-processed 790 EPWs. During this time our group demonstrated a real willingness to do whatever was needed to get the job done by voluntarily assisting with EPW sick call, handing out new clothing and cleaning up trash to reduce health and fire risks. The commander of the 403rd noted all of the activity and attitude, and additional help was brought in to assist us. Our enthusiasm was highly praised by Col. Novak. Our in-processing numbers continued to increase each day from 846 on Monday, 947 on Tuesday, 1,027 on Wednesday, 1,320 on Thursday, and 1,450 on Friday. For the first twelve-hours of Saturday we had processed about eight hundred when we were notified that our task was complete and we were released to return to Dhahran immediately.[131]"

131 Gilmore, Tad. LTC After Action Report (edited)

Dr. Gilmore and his group are to be commended for their actions. I was proud of them, as was Col Novak, who noted their abilities to General Schwarzkopf at his next visit. I passed along some of the more vivid stories about the EPW camp that were told to me directly from those who were there. An excerpt from one story that was published in *The Bismarck Tribune* is shown in the next chapter.

THE EPW PROCESSING TEAM:

Physicians: LTC Bruce T. (TAD) Gilmore, Officer in Charge
LTC Roger Allen
LTC John Wade
LTC Virgil Hayden
Maj. George Hsu
Maj. Norris (Pokey) Cleek

Medics:

SSG Kathy Hsu	SGT John Klinkhammer
SGT Robert Limon	SGT Tracy Roberts
SPC Sandy Coleman	SPC Jeffrey Fletcher
SPC Steve Layer	SPC Michael Livingston
SPC Robert Row	SPC Barry Wilson

"LTC Hayden recalls that on the EPW mission that they were flown to Dhahran and then they went by—but not to—the Khobar Towers.[132] They were able to see the building where the scud missile had hit and killed the National Guardsmen." (sic)[133] (see the text entry from February 25, 1991, in Chapter 6).

---

132 The Khobar Towers were a target a second time when struck by terrorist truck bombers in 1996. *Wikipedia*.

133 The unit, the 14th Quartermaster Detachment, was a United States Army Reserve water purification unit stationed in Greensburg, Pennsylvania

"One of the real problems was manning the processing center and completing the sick call. We had processed several English-speaking Iraqi physicians, and at our recommendation these doctors were divided among the various compounds. They were given some basic medical supplies and were soon in business. They were of tremendous assistance to the team. We soon convinced the powers that be to allow an emergency tent to be staffed by one of these physicians—noting the problem of having an EPW outside of the compound—but it worked out."

"The prisoners would first come into a small tent for a final search. They were allowed to keep money, religious artifacts, and some personal items. The only military item they were allowed to keep was their protective masks. They would then proceed to the next tent, where they would disrobe, placing their clothes in plastic bags. They would then go into the showers before coming into our tent for physical exams."

"One-third of the EPWs had injuries from what they called the Old War, which was the war between Iraq and Iran. Many of the wounds were from surgery or shrapnel. Another serious problem was their dental condition. Many of them had abscessed or rotting teeth. More than half of them had otitis externa, an infection of the outer ear canal. Many of them had eardrum perforations, which were probably due to the bombing that had occurred during the air war. Malnutrition was very common among them, but there were a number of troops who appeared to be well fed. We saw many people with ulcers and several with perforated ulcers. It was amazing that they could even function with all of the severe medical problems they had. I had come to realize that they were true soldiers after many of them said that this was not their war."

"The ages of the EPWs varied from as young as thirteen to as old as seventy. There was one group of Kurds that we processed that were at least in their fifties and sixties. One incident was notable. A jumpsuit that had been given to an EPW as new issue was orange/red in color and he would not put it on because, he told us, Saddam's troops dressed prisoners to be executed in red-colored shirts and this color was close enough. He was finally convinced that it would be ok to wear it. Then all of his friends wanted that color too. A lot of Iraqi soldiers were forced into serving in the Army by being threatened with reprisals against their families."[134]

George Hsu related a conversation he had had with Roger Allen, whose hobby was embroidery, one day when they were both relaxing after a hard day's work:

"The orders from higher up were that Kevlar and gas masks were to be carried at all times. All of us were aware of the orders, but of course we dumped our gear as soon as we got to the work area, as did all of the MPs. The Battalion Commander and the Command Sergeant Major toured the camp several times a day, very visibly wearing their Kevlar and carrying gas masks, but they never chided anyone else for not wearing theirs. One evening I was commenting to Roger about what a great representation of leadership this had been. 'They're wearing theirs because that's what they are told to do, but they don't enforce it because it's stupid,' I said.

---

134 Jacobsen. *A Story of the 311*[th]. p. 53–55 (edited)

"Roger looked up from his embroidery, thought for a second, and said, 'Well, George, it just goes to show that sometimes—sometimes, common sense will prevail over regulation.'"[135]

Although there was a fairly good in-depth monograph authored by West Point graduate, John Brinkerhoff et al.[136] regarding the use of Army Reservists in the processing of EPWs, including the 403rd MP Camp, I was disappointed that the study did not mention the contributions of the 311th team we sent to assist. Certainly our folks made a big difference in their in-processing numbers.

Above: 1991 Photo of Iraq EPW Camp, not necessarily Col. Novak's 403rd MP. In February desert nights are cold. Photo credit[137]

---

135 Hsu, Geo. Personal correspondence. 9/12/20012.
136 http://www.dtic.mil/cgi-bin/GetTRDoc?AD=ADA277768
137 http://waronterrornews.typepad.com/cgtwa/2012/08/iraqi-pows-circa-1991-where-are-they-now.html

CHAPTER 9
MARCH 2, 1991–17, 1991 (Eight day overlap)
Redeployment and Going Home

The Gulf War was like teenage sex. We got in too soon and
out too soon. —**Tom Harkin**

S aturday, March 2: *"I talked with Boatright. Kuwait City is out
as a re-deployment site. I suspect instead of re-deployment
there will be an early deployment home, but there is no
confirmation. I will fly to Riyadh on Tuesday to see what's up. The
logistics auditor is due down from Riyadh on Monday. According to
my section leaders there is a troop discipline problem. I told them
in a section leader meeting that I would support their collective
corrective actions whatever the problems or conduct violations
were and to put out the word that we were "cracking down". I
think most of the problems were minor celebrations that the war
was nearly over and they were anxious to go home. If their conduct
contributed to any delays in our departure I am sure they would*

regret it and told the section leaders to pass that information along as well.

Tuesday, March 5: "Roman and I left for Riyadh. It took ten hours on a C-130, mostly due to bad weather at KKMC. We puddle hopped in and were met by Boatright himself. The next day I talked with Col. B and Col. D.G. Tsoulos CENTCOM's (Central Command's) Medical Commander for Desert Storm. I repaired some fences. Boatright gave me a blouse for a desert battle dress uniform, and told me that we had three to four weeks to go home. The direct flight back in the C-130 cockpit took just one-and-a-half hours.

Saturday, March 9: "Col. Boatright called yesterday and gave us forty-eight hours' notice to go home. I had to pull logistics people off of the plane that was headed to Oman from Al Dhafra. The troops are happy. The logistics people are busy with problems getting sea-air containers. I hope not to have a rear detachment."

The above was my last diary entry. The most memorable things that happened during those last few days at AL Mafraq were:

- When the shooting was over and Iraq had surrendered, I was approached by one of Mafraq's staff physicians, who happened to be an Iraqi. The first words out of his mouth were, "Why didn't you guys finish the job?" I answered, "I don't know but I'll bet we'll be back within ten years." It was ten years and six months later when 9/11 became the most infamous date since December 7, 1941—Pearl Harbor.

- We had just hours to recover our EPW team from Kuwait. Fortunately, Col. Novak, Commander of the MP Camp, was available and he responded to our request immediately. They made it back with a couple of hours to spare.

- If it hadn't been for my on-the-ball Executive Officer, Jim Miller, we might have missed our flight home. Jim, having dealt with the 202's S-3 (operations) and S-4 (supply) officers the whole time was skeptical of their competence, and once again he was right. The 202nd kept insisting that we were to fly out of Bateen and they actually got peeved when Jim kept telling them that we were not on any Air Force Schedule out of Bateen. After several calls and frayed tempers—once again the 311th was a "pain in the arse"—Jim finally gave up on our Higher HQ and chased down our scheduled 747 flight on Dhahran's Departure Board. Dhahran, however, was six hundred miles away and our scheduled departure was just hours away. If we hadn't gotten there some other lucky outfit would have commandeered the Pam Am Charter and we would have been out of luck. Fortunately for us, Jim had some good-friend contacts at the American Embassy and the Air Force liaison officer at the Embassy finally called the 202nd direct and convinced them that our departure was from some other location. Meanwhile, anticipating a foul-up, he quietly arranged for standby buses and C130s. "It took seven C-130 Hercules cargo planes to load all eight hundred duffle bags, and four hundred Alice packs and troops to get us all there over a period of six to eight hours. The first flight left Abu Dhabi at approximately 1300 hours on March 10th, 1991 and the flight took one hour and twenty minutes."[138]

- We did need a rear detachment to take care of our equipment. I left the detail in the good hands of Major Tom Rowekamp and CWO Larry Cook.

From Jacobsen: "Our flight from Dhahran went directly to Rome, Italy. We landed about 0320 local time (March 11, 1991). Departing Rome at 0520, we flew directly to the USA via Canada. When we crossed the Canadian border, the chief flight attendant sang Lee Greenwood's 'God Bless the USA' and practically the whole unit was in tears."[139]

An aircraft fire at Kennedy Airport delayed our flight to Volk field in Wisconsin, but we finally arrived about 1530 on March 11, 1991,to be met by General Bagley himself. It took five days to out-process and that was possible only due to having gotten a waiver for audiometer hearing tests which we could complete at home stations. On March 16th we departed Fort McCoy on three separate buses, one for each city: Fargo, Minot, and Bismarck. "At one point west of Jamestown, a lone State Highway Patrolman stood at attention and saluted the buses as we drove by."[140]

Our homecoming was exceptional not only for us but also throughout the country, for all of the returning service men and women. There were parades and speeches, yellow ribbons everywhere, and crowds lining the streets applauding and waving

---

138 Jacobsen "A Story of the 311th-"p56
139 Ibid. p 58
140 Ibid. p 59.

flags. It was a far cry from the days of Viet Nam, and I hoped it erased the stigma of those times and helped heal the country of those wounds.

Home from the war, registered nurse, Capt. Melodee Grenz has a tearful reunion with her husband Dan Privatsky and six month old daughter, Brianna, March 16, 1991.

A Tale of war from those who were there

By Karen Hilfer Tribune Staff Writer
Hostilities were still part of the future when the 311th Army Evacuation Hospital flew out of the United States, but were realty by the time it landed in the United Arab Emirates.

"They were lost for a time and didn't even know it," said Linda Hook, wife of Col. William Hook, commander of the 3llth.

Once the bombing began, Linda said she tried to track the 311th's progress through the Military World tracer. She said they lost track of the plane at Spain and then the news reported a plane down.

"That was very, very scary," said Linda. "It was one of my worst nights. I just wanted to know the plane was on the ground." Relaxed, but still tired from the time change, Hook Saturday talked about the 311th's adventures during Desert Storm.

"If anything we were

Hook Relaxed.

overprepared for what we saw," he said. "I never worried about our medical skills."

The unit, which returned Friday, did have to do,some refresheer work on biological and chemical warfare training, becoming certified with gas masks and even qualifying on weapons.

Stationed in a hospital in Abu Dhabi, the 311th arrived anxious to get going and do things, said Hook. But their location was 400 miles from any fighting.

They quickly settled into the idea that they were a support mission and began integrating with the local medical community.

"Initially there was some jealousy and fear," said Hook. "There had been rumors that the Americans were coming in and going to take their jobs."

Once that obstacle was overcome, cooperation grew and the unit even has a standing invitation to come back.

"Diplomatically, we were a great success," said Hook. "Our kids worked so hard."

They spent hours on medical education with local medical personnel. Medical standards aren't as high as in the United States and something as fundamental as cardiopulmonary resusitation isn't part of the normal training ,said Hook.

Their success wasn't only pro-

fessionally, it was socially.

" There were a lot of tears when we left," said Hook. "Tears from us and them."

Once the ground fighting started, 16 members of the 311th went to camps to help screen the mounting number of Iraqi prisoners. On an average day those six doctors and 10 medics processed 900 people and up to 1300 on their busiest day.

Troops guarding the prisoners did keep their humor. With prisoners seated in endless rows, guards attempted to teach prison- ers some English. Doctors arriving were treated to a chorus of "Good morning Doctor" from thousands of throats.

English les- sons even became a little whimsical. As doctors moved among the prison- ers, on cue, several large prisoner sec- tions mimicked an American TV commercial and shouted "tastes great" and"less filling".

Looking to the future, Hook an- ticipates the 311th will probably lose a few members.

"Lives were interupted which they wen't pre- pared for,' he said.

But largely it's a close-knit group and he believes most will stay.

Not everyone is home yet. Two members volun- teered to stay be- hind to watch over the shipping of the 311th equipment. They are expected home very soon.

Gratified with the public wel- come, Hook said he hopes it erases some of the stigma of the Viet Nam era. "They were the real heroes, not us", he said.

EPILOGUE
**Reflections and the Ten Commandments
of Muslim Diplomacy**

*By three methods we may learn wisdom: first, by reflection,
which is noblest; second, by imitation, which is easiest; and
third by experience, which is the bitterest.* —**Confucius**

*D*uring the C-130 flight to Dhahran and the subsequent,
longer 747 flight home, we all had time to reflect on our
experiences. Below are some of mine.

Reflections on the Arabs:

On working with the Arabs we came away with both good
and not-so-good impressions, as they likely did about us. On the
positive side, they were greatly appreciative of our knowledge
and experience. In the last few weeks they didn't hesitate to ask
for our help through consultations, especially after Cleek and
Hayden saved one of their wives. They also were appreciative of
our teaching skills, positive attitudes, and friendliness. We had a

standing invitation to return any time we wished. This conflicted a little with the rapidity in which UAE officials acted to get the Americans out of their country once the fighting was over.

They were generous in providing us with whatever we needed in terms of comforts, access to their equipment, and the exchange of information, as long as we respected their customs. One of their favorite expressions, which we came to use too, was "Mafi Mushkala" (a phonetic spelling), which meant "No problem." In Arabic, it is written ةلكشم دجوت ال. Their security forces were tireless in protecting our perimeter, and appreciative of our knowledge in that regard. Col Roman and 1st SGT Campbell were both decorated with U.A.E. Meritorious Service Medals for these skills.

On the negative side, I learned that we had to get any oral agreements down in writing and have them signed. Then when an agreement was violated—and this happened more than once such as covering the emergency room at certain times or on specific days and they would not show up—we would have the proof necessary to convince them of to what they had agreed. Note in Appendix G that an oral agreement was reached on January 23 but we did not get a signature until February 4 after we realized we had better do so.

The problem was, for example, the Arabs would agree to specific assignments for our doctors or theirs like only the admitting physician could write orders on the patient. Then we would make rounds on our patients and find the orders had been changed on a patient that one of our doctors had admitted. I think they were testing our oral agreement. Once the agreement was signed like the one in Appendix G, all we had to do was show the offending physician or Dr. Gohary a copy of the signed agreement and they had to concede their "mistake". The same thing occurred with our technologists or nurses drawing blood, or prescriptions being changed by their pharmacy.

We were also at a big disadvantage when prior USA personnel apparently negotiated the use of the Mafraq facilities with promises that were never put into writing by unknown people from both sides.

I am writing this amidst a backdrop of Mid-East violence against U.S. embassies in September of 2012. I wonder how many of these kinds of undocumented actions or agreements, if any, have been committed recently by members of our State Department. From what I've observed about the cultures in the Middle East, the Arab men appear to be much like our Native American Lakota Sioux in the nineteenth century. Both groups liked to "count coup"[141] and at least some Arabs would count coup against their brother if they could. How do I know this? I have had personal experience with two Egyptian brothers with whom I was in business in the States. I do not know if my business associates were Muslims.

I can appreciate this apparent quality about the culture, though, a lot more since doing the extensive research on the Moro Muslims of the Philippines for my last book *Never Subdued*. Today's diplomats and leaders could learn a lot by study-

---

141 The Random House College Dictionary definition, 1.a highly successful stroke, act, or move; a clever action or accomplishment.

ing Captain (later General) John (Black Jack) Pershing's dealings with the Moros in the early twentieth century. He knew that they respected the old Hammurabi and Old Testament Law of "an eye for an eye and a tooth for a tooth." He also knew that they considered appeasement to be a sign of weakness. If you broke Moro (Moro is a Spanish word for Islam) law, there would be instant punishment. This situation still persists in Islamic cultures today as in the case of the quick beheading of the Saudi-born Palestinian terrorist in Jeddah, in 1991. In 1902, when Pershing arrested a local Muslim Datu (tribal leader) for possessing a stolen U.S. Army rifle, he was visited by another Muslim leader who told him that the Datu was innocent because he had bought the rifle from thieves. Pershing told him to "prove it." The next morning, the bodies of two thieves were in front of Pershing's tent and he released the Datu. Thereafter, Pershing's best source of information was the appreciative Muslim.

Another element that affected Arab Muslim attitudes is best illustrated by my experience listening to a Muslim physician who had been assigned by Dr. Gohary to teach us some basic facts about the Muslim religion. These sessions were arranged at our request—we Americans being naturally curious. I don't remember discussing this with anyone else but there is no doubt that any one of the Americans who sat in that large conference room during his lectures became aware of the facts that A.) he didn't want to be there and B.) he was, or at least we perceived him to be, hostile, especially when our young innocent female soldiers asked questions. It finally dawned on me that the probable reason for his attitude was the fact that we were infidels, and unlike our Yankee girls, Arabic women for the most part do not ask questions. I then remembered that most of the Arab Muslims considered their Hebrew neighbors in Israel infidels too and that there was no mention of Israel in their news broadcasts, which were censored, or in their phone directories, and as far as they were concerned Israel did not exist.

Let me be clear: not all of the Arab Muslims were as rigid as our Islamic instructor, but it was easy to see in retrospect how easy it would be for a young Muslim to become what we call radicalized. If, as a youth, you are taught to reject any religion except your own and taught to accept certain passages in the Koran as literal truth, then you wind up hating infidels and believing that you should destroy them. Some of the same kind of thinking has occurred in the West as well. The Crusades are one example. If you look back at what has happened since Desert Storm, we have to convince our leaders of exactly what Israeli Prime Minister Benjamin Netanyahu has known for some time: the Muslim terrorists want to kill us. How many more ambassadors, diplomats, and service men and women have to give up their lives before we accept this? I am not saying that all Muslim's hate infidels—that's certainly not the case. But like what proved to be the case in Nazi Germany, all it takes for bad things to happen is for good people to do nothing.

So, how should we deal with these people in the twenty first century? My suggestions would be to take some lessons from Captain John Pershing's Philippine experience in 1902; perhaps you could call these the ten commandments of Muslim diplomacy.

1. Be Confident.

2. Record Agreements, with Signatures.

3. Use Measured Responses to Breaches of Agreement.

4. Keep your word.

5. Respect their laws.

6. Be Honest.

7. Support Your Allies.

8. Recruit Muslim Allies for Human Rights.

9. Be Resolute.

10. Trust USA Power. (In God we trust!).

Here are the rules in greater detail:

1. Be confident. Show no fear. Muslims respect confident authority. On the other hand, weakness is provocative and they will likely test it so that they can count coup.

2. If you don't have it, get any agreements in writing—signed, sealed and delivered— or at least have some kind of visual recording that will prove what was agreed upon. Make sure that the agreement is binding to any peaceful or democratic change in government or authority.

3. Stand up for your rights. U.S. embassies are U.S. territory. When embassies are established, the host nation is responsible for their safety. If the walls are breached, immediately react with a measured response, regardless of who is responsible. If it's just a physical breach, consider options; for example you could:

   A.) Expel the people in their embassy and their diplomats out of the States.

   B.) Freeze their assets.

   C.) Deny them foreign aid.

D.) If any U.S. citizen is hurt or killed, send our own assets into their territory to get the culprits. Back it up with force and mean it. Pershing did this with his (i.e., the USA's) right to travel anywhere in the Philippines he wished.

E.) Consider other options such as a naval blockade and no-fly zones.

If the Muslims know that a breach has occurred, they will expect an equally appropriate reaction.

4. Keep your word. Don't promise rewards or threaten punishment without meaning it. This includes statements like, "All options are on the table."

5. While you are in their territory, respect their laws. This means that you may have to squelch your right to free speech while you are there, but remember that our embassies are US territories and you can express your free speech from there.

6. Be honest without compromising U.S. security or intentions.

7. Let it be known that you support your allies to the point of waging war for them if necessary. They might be a similar such ally—as long as you have a signed agreement, that is.

8. Help good Muslims to get involved. Have clarity of purpose. Human rights are part of our nature. Let them know this. Get specific if they ask.

9. Emphasize your resolve.

10. Trust the might of your country. Our motto is still "In God we trust."

One of the most critical of these suggestions—or are they commandments?—is number four. If you read about the Philippine-American war, the abatement of the Bates agreement with certain Muslims resulted in disaster. So, let's learn something from history and not prove that "what is past is prologue."[142]

"What if," you may ask, "you get a signed agreement between two allies and then one of them attacks the other?"

The answer may seem obvious to some. You simply write into the agreement what would happen if they did that. Then apply rule four. Granted, there may be an obfuscation of who did what first, but that is why we have intelligence sources, and our policies should not limit or handicap them.

Reflections on the Americans:

I was glad I never had to worry about our medical skills. The 311th had as good of a staff as you will find in any teaching hospital in the U.S. I would trust my own life with any one of them. Likewise, our 311th support staff was excellent, they knew what they were doing, and they were experienced.

I thought about the food services and diet we followed for those months when we were overseas. We were coming home slimmer and better fit than we had been when we had arrived. Colonel Jacobsen put it this way:

"Food services were provided by Mafraq Hospital. They were contracted to furnish food for the 311th. Though the dietary ser-

---

142 Shakespeare *The Tempest*

vices cooks and helpers were mostly Pakistani[143], their idea of good food was totally foreign to those accustomed to Hardee's, McDonald's, Red lobster, and the Olive Garden, and most of all to American home cooking. Their meals consisted at first of red, yellow or green rice depending on which spice was used, mutton, chicken and some vegetables. Later, we were able to get some beef from Australia, water buffalo—rumor had it—and some fish. Breads were abundant mostly unleavened. There was a noted absence of pork. Our dietician, LTC Corliss Trom, made constant efforts to Americanize the food that was served. Friendly persuasion was the main tactic. Soon, a new item appeared on the daily menu. Especially memorable was the day we had spaghetti and tomato sauce. Then came hamburgers, French fries, and fried eggs."[144]

Jacobsen then went on to laud Corliss Trom for her efforts, and he included Mafraq's head chef, Rosario.

---

143 Pakistanis also performed housekeeping services for Mafraq. They wore blue jump suit uniforms causing us to be reminded of Smurfs and we called them that, but not in a derogatory fashion. We appreciated them a lot.

144 Jacobsen. *A Story of the 311*[th] (p. 24)

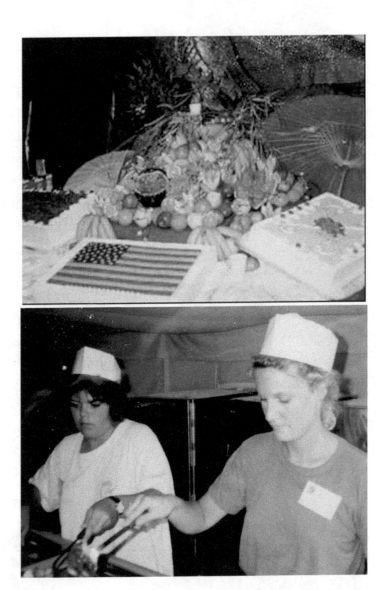

Above: 311th bakers and cooks were not idle. Hospital Food Service Specialists
PFCs Kerry Kraning and Mary Watt man the chow line.

Top photo: Rosario the Mafraq Chef and his crew.
Photo below: Dietician LTC Corliss Trom chatting with Executive Officer LTC Jim Miller.
Photo credits: Jacobsen & Hook

One of the reasons I was so confident about the 311ths competence involved the pharmacy. Although our preparation for overseas movement had allowed us to order drugs to fill our own formulary, we did not receive all of our supplies and push packages until February 24. Col. Jacobsen explains: "The pharmacy officers and twelve technicians worked well with the local staff of the hospital. We found that the practice of pharmacy in the hospital was all unsecured open-floor stock. The wards had to order the drugs that were required and then the pharmacy would fill a basket and send it back to the ward. There was little—if any—accounting of these drugs by the nursing units. Our technicians were able to work in several areas. The outpatient pharmacy filled all prescriptions for the clinic patients. The inpatient pharmacy filled all outpatient prescriptions when the OP pharmacy was closed, and they handled all of the drugs used within the hospital itself. There was also a pharmacy storeroom behind the main hospital building, within the main warehouse. All supplies were purchased on an annual basis.

"There were some inaccurate ordering procedures, which created shortages. Once out of a stock, an item would not be available for the rest of the year unless special arrangements were made.

"When we first arrived, the 311th members used the inpatient pharmacy for medications prescribed by our own doctors, but what was delivered was not always what was prescribed. Because of this, we set up our own pharmacy, and we dispensed and restocked the Sick Call Pharmacy with pre-packaged medications on a daily basis."[145]

So you see, I not only had confidence in our medical skills, but also in our pharmacy staff and other support staff as well, right down to the administration, the motor pool, the laundry, the armory, the postal service, nursing, food services, chaplains, NBC specialists, security, operations, supply logistics, etc. If I had ever had to go back to war, I would have felt blessed to be with such dedicated competent people again.

Above: Pharmacy staff members Col. John Jacobsen, SSG Kathy Perkerewicz, Capt. Jerry Wahl

---

145 Jacobsen. *A Story of the 311th* (edited). (p. 30 –31)

Some twenty-plus years have now gone by and a number of good people from the 311th have left this life. As we age there will be more and more. My own life expectancy at this point is well under twenty more years. I wish we could pass on our experience to the next generation through reflection, which Confucius says is the easiest. Perhaps some of our next leaders will imitate— the next best method of gaining wisdom—General Pershing and those like him who have at least partially succeeded in Muslim negotiations.

One good example of success from Desert Storm was Secretary of State Jim Baker's statement of resolve to Deputy Prime Minister of Iraq, Tariq Aziz, that we would use nuclear weapons if they used WMD. That flat-out warning was enough to prevent the use of those weapons and the Iraqis knew that we would keep our word.

Another example of success comes from Col. Tichenor speaking about our post war activities: "We flew missions out of Diego Garcia up to the Gulf and back just to let them know we were there as kind of a deterrent; that there were still B-52's in the area and you guys pay attention because we can bring them up any time we want."[146]

Let us hope and pray, as I stated in the epilogue to *Never Subdued*, referring to the Moros (Followers of Islam) of the Philippines: "the hope is that if they can control their own radicalized members to respect human rights and the laws of their nation(s), perhaps they can learn to live together with the rest of the human race. Otherwise, the world will eventually find a way to destroy

---

146 This book, chapter seven.

any group, no matter their religion or origin, that preys on the innocent or helpless."[147]

If the Muslim world doesn't make this level of control happen soon, then we'll all have to learn by Confucius's bitterest way—experience—and the next one will be the worst.

END

---

147 Hook, Franklin. *Never Subdued*. CreateSpace: Charleston, SC. 2011 (p. 344)

APPENDIX A
Colonel Hook's Administrative Staff:

LTC James R. Miller	Executive Officer, Immediate past commander
MSG Dale F. Rummel	Facility Chief 311th Evac Hospital (Did not deploy)
CSM Jerome M. Braxmeyer	Command Sergeant Major, 311th Evac Hospital
MAJ John T. Rowekamp	Chief Supply Officer
CAPT William C. Wood	Services Officer
SFC Rene LaSanta	Wardmaster
SFC Bruce D. Kirchmeier	Personnel Staff NCO
SGT David A. Becker	Admin Specialist
SFC Charles Zuspann	Unit Clerk
SSG JoAnn Cook	Patient Admin NCO
SSG Merle Grenz	Unit Supply SGT
SFC Richard Buell	Medical Supply SGT
SSG Noreen Bartlett	Legal Specialist

APPENDIX B
DEPLOYED KEY PERSONNEL:

Commander	COL William F. Hook
Exec Officer	LTC James R. Miller
S-2 (Intelligence) S-3 (Operations)	LTC Helen Johnson
Command Sgt Major	CSM Jerry Braxmeyer
Unit Troop Commander	MAJ Robert O. Black
First Sergeant	1SG Jeff Campbell
Ass't 1st Sgt	SFC Gary Kuch
Personnel	COL Gil Roman
Chief Supply & Services	MAJ Tom Rowekamp
Hospital Dietician	LTC Corliss Trom
Patient Admin	MAJ Terry Paulson
Chief Professional Services	COL Gerry Moyer
Chief Surgery	COL. Don Bishop
Chief Medicine	MAJ Barry Graham
Chief Nurse	COL. Jane Giedt
Assis't Chief Nurse	LTC Suzanne LeClaire
Chief Anesthesiology	LTC Bob Brunsvold[148]
Chief OR Nurse	MAJ. Diana Hamilton
Chief Wardmaster	SFC Rene LaSanta
Chief Pharmacist	COL John Jacobsen
Chief Dental Services	COL Carney Middleton[149]
Weapons	CW3 Larry Cook

---

148 Brunsvold's MOSQ was 61J (Gen Surgery) but he is certified in Anesthesiology as well.

149 The 311th had no dental equipment, so Middleton assigned himself to the Air Force Dental Corps at Al Dhafra for the duration.

APPENDIX C
Alphabetical Roster of the 311th 3/March/1991:

SOLDIER	RANK	MOSQ	DESIGNATION
Adams, Jay R.	SSG	Practical Nurse, Medic	91C3O
Adams, Sheryl	SSG	OR Specialist	91D3O
Akason, Gregory D.	SGT	Medical Supply Specialist	76J2O
Alexander, Frances C.	SSG	OR Specialist	91D3O
Allen, Roger L.	LTC	Field Surgeon	62B00
Allen, Susan M.	LTC	Medical-Surgical Nurse	66H00
Anda, Michael J.	SPC	Patient Admin Specialist	71G1O
Andersh, Davonne L.	SGT	Orthopedic Specialist	91H2O
Anderson, Benjamin L.	SGT	OR Specialist	91D2O
Anderson, Eric W.	SGT	Respiratory Specialist	91V2O
Anderson, Kip W.	SSG	Pharmacy Specialist	91Q3O
Anderson, Tamie K.	SPC	Chaplain Assistant	71M1O
Andvik, Parry M.	SPV	Pharmacy Specialist	91Q1O
Archer, John T.	SGT	Hospital Food Service Sp'lst	91M1O
Ariegwe, Kingsley U.	PFC	Medical Specialist	91A1O
Aune, Jane E.	SPC	Administrative Specialist	71L1O
Bakken, Robert K.	SGT	Medical Specialist	91A1O
Bales, Sandra	SPC	Equipment Records Specialist	76C10
Balko Barbara L.	1LT	Medical Surgical Nurse	66H00
Bartlett, Noreen L.	SSG	Legal Specialist	71D3O
Bata, Bonnie R.	CPT	Medical-Surgical Nurse	66H00
Becker, David A.	SGT	Administrative Specialist	71L2O
Beehler, Nora	PFC	Unknown, soldier transferred	

Belgarde, Michael J.	SPC	Chemical Operations Sp'lst	54B1O
Bell, Brenda K.	SGT	OR Specialist	91D2O
Bishop, Don L.	COL	Orthopedic Surgeon	61M00
Black, Robert O.	MAJ	Medical Service Corps Unit Cdr.	67F00
Blatnick, Robert A.	PFC	OR Specialist	91D1O
Blea, Patrick	SSG	OR Specialist	91D3O
Bohl, Anthony J.	PFC	Medical Lab Specialist	92B1O
Bollinger, Leroy G.	SFC	Chemical Operations Sp'lst	54B4O
Bondley, Dianne M	2LT	Medical-Surgical Nurse	66H00
Braaten Gail	1LT	Medical Surgical Nurse	66H00
Braun, James A.	SPC	Medical Supply Specialist	76J1O
Braxmeyer, Jerome L.	CSM	Command Sergeant Major	00Z5O
Bridwell, Janet K.	SSG	Pharmacy Specialist	91Q3O
Brooks, David O.	CPT	Field Medical Assistant NBC	67B3R[150]
Brower, James G.	SGT	OR Specialist	91D2O
Brown, Jerry R.	SFC	Tactical Commo Chief	31G4O
Brown, Ronald C.	1LT	Medical Surgical Nurse	66H00
Brudvik, Celine, L.	2LT	Medical-Surgical Nurse	66H00
Brunsvold, Robert A.	LTC	Surgeon, Anesthesiologist[151]	61J00
Buck, Jacquelyn J.	SGT	Pharmacy Specialist	91Q2O
Buechler, David R.	SPC	Medical Specialist	91A1O
Buell, Richard W.	SFC	Medical Supply Specialist	76J4O
Burr, Angela J.	SPC	Practical Nurse, Medic	91C2O
Byre, Eric A.	SPC	Medical lab Specialist	92B1O
Calbart, Ellen D.	SPC	Unit Supply Specialist	76Y1O

---

150 The "R" stands for "radiation" in this Nuclear, Biological, and Chemical warfare trained officer.

151 Dr. Brunsvold's MOS was for a surgeon, but he was a board-certified anesthesiologist.

Campbell, Jeffrey W.	1SGT	Medical NCO	91B5M
Casey, Kathleen A.	CPT	Medical-Surgical Nurse	66H00
Cavalier, Curtis L.	1LT	Medical-Surgical Nurse	66H00
Christiansen, Gail A.	CPT	Clinical Nurse	66J00
Cleek, Norris E.	MAJ	General Surgeon	61J00
Cobble, Nancy A.	LTC	Psychiatric Nurse	66C00
Coleman, Sandy L.	PFC	Medical Specialist	91A1O
Connnors, Joseph I. III	SPC	Administrative Specialist	71L1O
Cook, Joanne M	SSG	Patient Administration Sp'lst	71G1O
Cook, Larry J	CW3	Automotive Maintenance WO	915A0
Czernek, Peter	MAJ	Internist	61F00
Darko, Sternell	SFC	Practical Nurse, Medic	91C4O
Davidson, Bruce L.	1LT	Medical-Surgical Nurse	66H00
Degenstein, Roger D.	SSG	OR Specialist	91D3O
Dennis, Delbert S.	SSG	Medical-Surgical Nurse	91C3O
Desplenter, Michael A.	SPC	Telecommunications Operator	74C1O
Dehne, Kevin L.	PV2	OR Specialist	91D1O
Deibert, Renee	PFC	Laundry and Bath Specialist	57E1O
Derheim, Michael M.	SPC	Medical Specialist	91A1O
Dickason, Timothy j.	SPC	Medical Lab Specialist	92B1O
Dieken, Holly	MAJ	Dietician (transferred)	65C00
Dietz, Clark A.	SPC	Hospital Food Service Sp'lst	91M1O
Dilbeck, Kyle L.	SGT	Medical Supply Specialist	76J2O
Dooley, Nereus J.	PFC	OR Specialist	91D1O
Dunham, Joni R	SGT	OR Specialist	91D2O
Dunki, Carolyn M.	MAJ	Medical Surgical Nurse	66H00
Duran, William R.	PV2	Generator Repairman	52F1O
Dyise, Tilly L.	PFC	Medical Supply Specialist	76J1o
Ebel, James A.	SSG	Practical Nurse, Medic	91C3O

Ebel, Kimberly S.	SPC	Medical Specialist	91A1O
Eberhardt, Karen L.	LTC	Medical-Surgical Nurse	66H00
Eckert, Douglas A.	SGT	OR Specialist	91D3O
Edwards, Michael	PFC	Light Wheel Vehicle Mechanic	63B1O
Egan, Mary E.	SGT	Practical Nurse, Medic	91C2O
Eklund, Larry L	PFC	Medical Specialist	91A1O
Elker, Kevin D	SPC	Hospital Food Service Sp'lst	91M1O
Ellis, Patricia	CAPT	Operating Room Nurse	66E00
Emerson, Jennifer L.	SPC	Laundry and Bath Specialist	57E1O
Engel, Troy A.	SGT	Pharmacy Specialist	91Q2O
Ensz, Timmy D.	SPC	Utilities Equipment Repair	52C1O
Evanger, Kirby L.	PFC	Administrative Specialist	71L2O
Fahlstrom Brian C.	SGT	Medical Specialist	91A1O
Faleski, Edward	LTC	Radiologist	61R00
Feldt, Peggy A.	2LT	Medical-Surgical Nurse	66H00
Ferch, Anne G.	PFC	Medical Supply Specialist	76J1O
Fessler, Shari B.	CPT	Medical Surgical Nurse	66H00
Fiechtner, Kari C.	SGT	Pharmacy Specialist	91Q2O
Finnegan Kathleen L.	SPC	Medical Supply Specialist	76J1O
Fitterer, Alvin S.	SPC	Quartermaster Chemical Equip	63J1O
Fletcher, Jeffrey M.	SPC	Medical Specialist	91A1O
Franson, Mark A.	1LT	Medical-Surgical Nurse	66H00
Fry, Harvey P. III	2LT	Medical-Surgical Nurse	66H00
Fryman, Michael P.	1LT	Medical-Surgical Nurse	66H00
Gaughan, Shawn T.	SGT	Practical Nurse, Medic	91C2O
Garrett, Sonny	SGT	unknown transferred after	1-9
Gee, Chad C.	SPC	Medical Specialist	91A1O
Giedt, Douglas	LTC	Nurse Anesthetist	66F00
Giedt, Jane P.	COL	Medical-Surgical Nurse	66H00

Gieser[152], Jeffry M.	SGT	OR Specialist	91D2O
Gilchrist, Brian f.	CPT	General Surgeon[153]	61M00
Gilmore, Bruce T.	LTC	General Surgeon	61J00
Gitlin, David	1LT	Medical-Surgical Nurse	66H00
Glaser, Jeffrey M.	SPC	Utilities Equipment Repair	52C1O
Glatt, Ronny A.	SPC	Equipment Records, Parts	76C1O
Goecke, Paul R.	SSG	Patient Administration Sp'lst	71G3O
Goodrun, Ronnie O.	SPC	Medical Specialist	91A1O
Gooselaw, Brett J.	SPC	Medical Specialist	91A1O
Gorthy, Shawn J.	PFC	OR Specialist	91D1O
Graham, Barry A.	MAJ	Internist	61F00
Grenz, Melodee J.	CPT	Medical-Surgical Nurse	66H00
Grenz, Merle D.	SSG	Unit Supply Specialist	76Y3O
Gronland, Larry D.	MAJ	Nurse Anesthetist	66F00
Groothius, Holly J.	PV2	Medical Specialist	91A1O
Hagen, Terry M.	SFC	Hospital Food Service Sp'lst	91M4O
Hagle, James M.	SSG	Hospital Food Service Sp'lst	91M3O
Hagle, Robert J.	SPC	Hospital Food Service Sp'lst	91M1O
Haider, Mark A.	SPC	Medical Lab Specialist	92B1O
Hall, Jeremy P.	PV2	Laundry and Bath Specialist	57E1O
Hamalainen, Roger E.	PFC	Psychiatric Specialist	91F1O
Hamilton, Diana L.	MAJ	OR Nurse	66E00
Hammersky, Raeanna	SPC	Medical Specialist	91A1O
Hammett, Wanda J.	SSG	Practical Nurse, Medic	91C3O
Hancock, Chad J.	PV2	Unit Supply Specialist	76Y1O

---

152 Spelled Geiser on a previous roster
153 DR. Gilchrist was a General Surgeon in an orthopedic slot because of our orthopedic shortages.

Hanson, Arlen K.	SSG	Patient Administration Sp'lst	71G3O
Hatfield, Michelle G	PFC	Hospital Food Service Sp'lst	91M1O
Hauck, Marisa A.	PFC	Laundry and Bath Specialist	57E1O
Haugen, Arthur C. Jr.	CPT	Pharmacy Officer	68H00
Hawkes, Stephanie L.	1LT	Medical-Surgical Nurse	66H00
Hayden, Virgil L.	LTC	OB-GYN Surgeon	66J00
Hedlund, Pal D.	PFC	Patient Administration Sp'lst	71G1O
Heinz, Dale S.	SPC	Medical Specialist	91A1O
Heiser, Mary F.	PFC	Medical Supply Specialist	76J1O
Henry, Sarah K.	SGT	Medical Lab Specialist	92B2O
Hertz. Ricky L.	SPC	Hospital Food Service Sp'lst	91M1O
Herzog, Wendy K.	SPC	OR Specialist	91D1O
Hiller, Travis W.	SGT	OR Specialist	91D2O
Hoerer, Charles M.	SPC	Medical Lab Specialist	92B1O
Hoffman, Daniel W.	SSG	X-Ray Specialist	91P30
Hoffmann, Beva Jean V.	SGT	Medical Supply Specialist	76J2O
Hogart Michelle M.	SGT	Practical Nurse, Medic	91C2O
Hohn, James V.	SPC	Practical Nurse, Medic	91C1O
Hohn. William R.	SSG	Hospital Food Service Sp'lst	91M3O
Holdkraft, Kaylene F.	SGT	Practical Nurse, Medic	91C2O
Holt, Carl E.	SSG	Administrative Specialist	71L3O
Holter, Jay D	SSG	Practical Nurse, Medic	91C3O
Holter, Kara M.	SSG	Patient Administration Sp'lst	71G2O
Hook, William F.	COL	Radiologist	61R00
Horner, Melvina J.	SPC	Single Channel Radio Operator	31C1O
Houghton-Burciaga, Cynthia A.	SGT	Practical Nurse, Medic	91C3O
Houle, Frederick J.	SPC	OR Specialist	91D1O
Howard, Gary R.	MAJ	Clinical Lab Officer	66F00
Hsu, George S.	MAJ	Internist	61F00

Hsu, Kathleen Ann B.	SSG	Practical Nurse, Medic	91C3O
Hutchinson, Linda W.	SSG	Practical Nurse, Medic	91C3O
Inman, Timothy J.	SGT	Practical Nurse, Medic	91C3O
Jackson, St. Clair A.	SPC	Medical Lab Specialist	92B1O
Jacobs, Todd S.	SPC	Hospital Food Service Sp'lst	91M1O
Jacobsen, John L.	COL	Pharmacist	68H00
Jacobson[154], Miles C.	SPC	OR Specialist	91D1O
James, Michael T.	SPC	Medical Specialist	91A1O
Janezinch, Glenn A.	SSG	Medical Lab Specialist	92B3O
Jeffrey, Harry E.	PV2	Medical Specialist	91A1O
Jess, John M.	SGT	Food Service Specialist	94B2O
Johnson, Helen D.	LTC	Medical-Surgical Nurse	66H00
Johnson, Judith	2LT	Medical-Surgical Nurse	66H00
Johnson, Marc A.	SPC	Practical Nurse, Medic	91C1O
Johnson, Sean D.	PFC	Practical Nurse, Medic	91C3O
Kallias, Larry J.	SFC	Practical Nurse, Medic	91C4O
Keeney, David L.	SGT	Hospital Food Service Sp'lst	91M2O
Kempfer, Florene C	1LT	Medical-Surgical Nurse	66H00
Kempton, Marcia E.	CPT	Medical-Surgical Nurse	66H00
Kendly Edward L.	SSG	OR Specialist	91D3O
Kilen, Keith, L.	PFC	Utilities Equipment Repair	52C1O
Kilen, Orletta, L.	MAJ	Medical-Surgical Nurse	66H00
King, Paul T.	PFC	Medical Lab Specialist	92B1O
King, Richard D	SFC	Respiratory Specialist	91V2O
Kirchmeier, Bruce D.	SFC	Personnel Sergeant	75Z4O
Kerklie, Kenneth R.	PV2	Excess in MOS transferred after	1-9-
Klinkhammer, John J.	SGT	Practical Nurse, Medic	91C2O

154 Spelled Jacobsen on a previous roster

Klug, Elizabeth A.	SPC	Administrative Specialist	71L1O
Knaust, Tammy A.	SPC	Medical Specialist	91A1O
Koch, Nancy J.	PV2	Medical Specialist	91A1O
Kramer, Dwayne	SFC	Light Wheel Vehicle Mechanic	63B4O
Kramer, Randy E.	SGT	Laundry and Bath Specialist	57E2O
Kraning, Kerry A.	PFC	Hospital Food Service Sp'lst	91M1O
Krein, Karen K.	SGT	Patient Administration Sp'lst	71G2O
Kreig, Peter A.	SGT	Medical Specialist	91A2O
Kuchta, Patricia	SFC	Practical Nurse, Medic	91C4O
Kuck, Gary L.	SFC	Respiratory Specialist	91V2O
Kula, Gordon J.	SGT	X-Ray Specialist	91P2O
Kulzer, Carmen M.	PFC	Medical Specialist	91A1O
Lambert, Jean M.	SPC	Hospital Food Service Sp'lst	91M1O
Larison, David	SPC	Medical Specialist	91A1O
Larson, Patricia A.	SPC	Administrative Specialist	71L1O
LaSanta, Rene S.	SFC	Practical Nurse, Medic	91C4O
Layer, Steven F.	SPV	Medical Specialist	91A1O
LeClaire, Suzanne M.	LTC	Medical-Surgical Nurse	66H00
Lee, Robert M.	SPC	Medical Specialist	91A1O
Leingang, Robyn M.	SPC	Administrative Specialist	71L1O
Lew, Sylvia A.	SSG	X-Ray Specialist	91P3O
Leyba, Gregory J.	SGT	OR Specialist	91D2O
Limon, Robert Jr.	SGT	Medical Specialist	91A2O
Lindberg, Franklin D.	SPC	Patient Administration Sp'lst	71G1O
Lindberg, Michelle R.	2LT	Medical-Surgical Nurse	66H00
Little, Paul C.	SSG	Practical Nurse, Medic	91C3O
Livingston, Michael B.	SPC	Practical Nurse, Medic	91C1O
Logan, Dennis B.	2LT	Medical-Surgical Nurse	66H00
Logan, Judith M.	2LT	OR Nurse	66E00

Lomsdal, Ronnie L.	CPT	Internist	66F00
Loomis, Lawrence D.	SFC	Practical Nurse, Medic	91C4O
Lucy Gerald B.	SSG	OR Specialist	91D2O
Lunde, Brenda	SPC	Medical Specialist	91A1O
Lunghofer, Sherry L	SPC	Medical Specialist	91A1O
Lupien, Marcia R.	MAJ	Medical-Surgical Nurse	66H00
Lyman, Larry E.	SGT	Hospital Food Service Sp'lst	91M1O
Magee, Lisa M.	SSG	Practical Nurse, Medic	91C3O
Mahler, Dean A.	MAJ	Clinical Lab Officer	68f00
Mahoney, Patrick G.	PV2	Generator Repairman	52F1O
Mahurin, Kathy S.	SSG	Practical Nurse, Medic	91C3O
Mallon, Dawn M.	SPC	Medical Specialist	91A1O
Maragos, Gerald. B	SGT	OR Specialist	91D2O
Marquart, Lawrence	SSG	Utilities Equipment Repair	52C3O
Mayer, Louvicia E.	1LT	Medical-Surgical Nurse	66H00
McBride, Casey M.	SGT	Practical Nurse, Medic	91C2O
McClure, Lisa A.	SGT	Pharmacy Specialist	91Q2O
McCullough, William C	PFC	Light Wheel Vehicle Mechanic	63B1O
McDaniel, Sandy R.	SPC	X-Ray Specialist	91P1O
McDougall, Rebecca E.	CPT	OR Nurse	66E00
McGregor, Steven J.	PFC	OR Specialist	91D1O
McKaig, Katherine A.	1LT	Medical-Surgical Nurse	66H00
McMillan, Shirley A.	CPT	Medical-Surgical Nurse	66H00
Meakin, Christine A	SPC	OR Specialist	91D1O
Mertz, Stacy J.	SPC	Unit Supply Specialist	76Y1O
Meyer, Thomas C.	2LT	Medical-Surgical Nurse	66H00
Middleton, Carney M.	COL	Dentistry, General	63A00
Miller, Angela	PFC	Excess in MOS transferred after	1-9
Miller, James R.	LTC	Field Medical Assistant MSC	67B00

Mitlying, Dawn E.	1LT	Medical-Surgical Nurse	66H00
Mitzel, Frederick	MAJ	Medical-Surgical Nurse	66H00
Mjoen, Jodi J.	SPC	Medical Specialist	91A1O
Moe, Randy S.	SPC	OR Specialist	91D1O
Mohr, Joseph A.	SFC	Practical Nurse, Medic	91C4O
Monette, Walter J.	SGT	Light Wheel Vehicle Mechanic	63B2O
Morgan Thomas C.	MAJ	Internist	66F00
Morgan, Wendi	SPC	unknown probably transferred after 1-9	
Mosbrucker, Calvin K.	SPC	Bio Medical Equip.Specialist	35G1O
Mott, Corey J.	SPC	Combat Signaler	31K1O
Moyer, Gerald B.	COL	General Surgeon	61J00
Mueller, Henry A.	SFC	Special Equipment Repair	52X4O
Murchie, Ann M.	SFC	Practical Nurse, Medic	91C4O
Muth, Alexander W.	PFC	Medical Specialist	91A1O
Nabben, Dale V.	1LT	Chaplain	56A00
Nachand, Christopher, D.	SPC	Medical Specialist	91A1O
Nall, David E.	SPC	Medical Specialist	91A1O
Narum, Daryk H.	SPC	Medical Supply Specialist	76J1O
Nathan, Tracy, A.	PFC	Laundry and Bath Specialist	57E1O
Naumann, Karl F.	SGT	Pharmacy Specialist	91Q2O
Naumann, Richard A.	CPT	Medical-Surgical Nurse	66H00
Neer, Allen L.	SGT	Combat Signaler	31K2O
Nelson, Chad A.	PFC	Medical Supply Specialist	76J1O
Nelson, Chad M.	SPC	Pharmacy Specialist	91Q1O
Nelson Christina L.	SPC	Medical Specialist	91A1O
Nelson, Deborah J.	1LT	Medical-Surgical Nurse	66H00
Nelson, Deborah J.	1LT	Medical-Surgical Nurse	66H00
Nigg, Lee C.	SSG	Medical Lab Specialist	92B3O
Norling, Arland E.	SFC	Practical Nurse, Medic	91C4O

Novotny, Eric A.	PV2	Patient Administration Sp'lst	71G1O
Nunziato, Michael	SGT	Medical Supply Specialist	76J1O
O'Donnell, Michael T. Jr.	SPC	Medical Specialist	91A1O
O'Keefe, Thomas L.	2LT	Medical-Surgical Nurse	66H00
Olson, Angela J.	PFC	OR Specialist	91D1O
Olson Brent L.	SPC	Medical Supply Specialist	76J1O
Olson, Dean J.	SGT	Respiratory Specialist	91V2O
O'Neal, Terri Z.	SSG	Practical Nurse, Medic	91C3O
Osborn, Steven C.	2LT	Medical-Surgical Nurse	66H00
Osborne, Sheila A.	PFC	OR Specialist	91D1O
Oster, Karen A.	SPC	X-Ray Specialist	91P1O
Palardy, Tammy L.	1LT	Medical-Surgical Nurse	66H00
Parmelee, Alexander	PFC	unknown probably transferred after 1-9	
Patterson, Cheryl B.	SSG	Administrative Specialist	71L3O
Paul, Anthony J.	SGT	Laundry and Bath Specialist	57E2O
Paulson, Scott A.	SPC	Combat Signaler	31K1O
Paulson, Terry T.	MAJ	Patient Administration	67E00
Pedersen, Sandra J.	1LT	Medical-Surgical Nurse	66H00
Perius, Nicholas J.	2LT	Medical-Surgical Nurse	66H00
Perkerewicz, Kathleen M.	SSG	Pharmacy Specialist	91Q3O
Perry, Travis T.	SPC	Cardiac Specialist	91N1O
Peterson, Eugene G.	COL	Ophthalmologist	60S00
Peterson, Margo l.	1LT	Medical-Surgical Nurse	**66H00**
Peuser, Carol J.	SGT	Pharmacy Specialist	91Q20O
Pippen, Penelope K.	SPC	Patient Administration Sp'lst	71G1O
Plummer, James R.	PFC	OR Specialist	91D1O
Polansky, Dale B.	SPC	Psychiatric Specialist	91F1O
Poling, Maria M.	SPC	Medical Specialist	91A1O
Prescott, Chad M.	PFC	Telecommunications Operator	74C1O

Puhr, Robyn M.	PFC	OR Specialist	91D1O
Rada, Delfin A.	MAJ	Internist	61F00
Rasset, Timothy P.	SSG	Hospital Food Service Sp'lst	91M3O
Rayburn, Terri L.	PFC	Medical Supply Specialist	76J1O
Reese, Gregory H. Jr.	CPT	Medical-Surgical Nurse	66H00
Reese, Paul F.	SFC	Practical Nurse, Medic	91C4O
Rettinger, David A.	SGT	OR Specialist	91D2O
Robertson, Tracy A.	SGT	Practical Nurse, Medic	91C2O
Roed, Nicola J.	1LT	Medical-Surgical Nurse	66H00
Roe, Robert C.	SPC	Medical Specialist	91A1O
Rogers, Diana L.	PFC	Medical Supply Specialist	76J1O
Roman, Gilbert D.	COL	Health Services Material MSC	67K00
Rosada-Gonzolez, C.	SSG	Pharmacy Specialist	91Q3O
Roth, Stephanie A.	SPC	Medical Specialist	91A1O
Rowekamp, John T.	MAJ	Field Medical Assistant MSC	67B00
Rudnick, Robert F.	SSG	Patient Administration Sp'lst	71G3O
Ruhnke, Brenda	SPC	unknown soldier transferred after 1-9	
Ruhnke, Tammy L.	SPC	Chaplain Assistant	71M1O
Ruhoff, Steven D.	SGT	Laundry and Bath Specialist	57E2O
Sailer, Craig A.	SGT	OR Specialist	91D2O
Sandberg, James C.	PFC	Medical Specialist	91A1O
Santos, Igmidio A.	MAJ	Psychiatrist	60W00
Sather, Gary P.	SPC	Medical Supply Specialist	76J1O
Schaffer, Cheri J	2LT	Medical-Surgical Nurse	66H00
Scharmer, Kristi L.	CPT	Medical-Surgical Nurse	66H00
Scherr, Terry L.	SGT	Utilities Equipment Repairer	52C2O
Schmitz, Carol A.	2LT	Medical-Surgical Nurse	66H00

Seibert, Richard D[155].	SFC	Practical Nurse, Medic	91C4O
Seiler, Brian L.	PFC	Generator Repairman	52D1O
Shanahan, John P.	1LT	Operating Room Nurse	66E00
Shearer, Robert L.	SPC	Practical Nurse, Medic	91C2O
Shull, Ruth A.	LTC	Medical-Surgical Nurse	66H00
Simdorn, Darlene J.	LTC	Medical-Surgical Nurse	66H00
Simon, Donna R.	SGT	Laundry and Bath Specialist	57E2O
Sivertson, Todd A.	SGT	Practical Nurse, Medic	91C3O
Spiegel,[156] Phil	COL	Orthopedic Surgeon	61M00
Stacy, Carolyn R.	PFC	Medical Specialist	91A1O
Stahl, Kyle J.	PFC	Medical Lab Specialist	92B1O
Steffen, Elizabeth M.	SSG	Practical Nurse, Medic	91C3O
Stelter, Darian L.	SPC	Light Wheel Vehicle Mechanic	63B1O
Stevenson, Joel A.	SPC	Hospital Food Service Sp'lst	91M1O
Stockert, Susan A.	SPC	Medical Supply Specialist	76J1O
Stone Nelson C.	MAJ	Chaplain	56A00
Stute, Sharon	MAJ	Medical-Surgical Nurse	66H00
Sullivan, Merle R.	SPC	Practical Nurse, Medic	91C2O
Sutton, Kristina L.	1LT	Operating Room Nurse	66E00
Sveum, Heather A.	PFC	Medical Specialist	91A1O
Swalstad, Wanda R.	SPC	Patient Administration Sp'lst	71G1O
Swanson, Karen L.	2LT	Medical-Surgical Nurse	66H00
Swedberg, Kathy A.	SGT	Patient Administration Sp'lst	71G2O
Tapia, Fred Jr.	SPC	Medical Specialist	91A1O
Tavary Anne M.	SPC	Psychiatric Specialist	91F1O
Ternes, Lynn M.	PFC	Medical Specialist	91A1O

155 Spelled Siebert on a previous roster
156 Transferred before deployment

Tessmer, Larry D.	CW3	Physician's Assistant	60A00
Thibert, Jerry L.	SPC	Medical Specialist	91A1O
Thomas Herbert J. III	MAJ	Orthopedic Surgeon	61M00
Thompson, Carol J.	SGT	Dental Specialist	91E1O
Thompson, Mary E.	SFC	Practical Nurse, Medic	91C4O
Thompson, Patrick A.	SPC	Light Wheel Vehicle Mechanic	63B1O
Tinsley, Kimberly M.	SPC	Practical Nurse, Medic	91C2O
Tobiness, Terry B.	SFC	Practical Nurse, Medic	91C3O
Tom, Linda L.	CPT	Medical-Surgical Nurse	66H00
Torgerson, Katheryn M.	SGT	Medical Lab Specialist	92B3O
Trom, Corliss, L.	LTC	Hospital Dietician	65C00
Tutty, Thomas W.	SPC	Practical Nurse, Medic	91C2O
Tweeden, Betty J.	SPC	Medical Specialist	91A1O
Varner, Bradley J.	SGT	Practical Nurse, Medic	91C3O
Vick, Robert S.	SSG	Radio Operator	31C3O
Victorson, Thomas C.	CPT	Medical-Surgical Nurse	66H00
Vinger, Grant D.	SSG	OR Specialist	91D3O
Voeller, Dennis D	SSG	Administrative Specialist	71L3O
Voll, Janelle M.	SGT	Medical Lab Specialist	92B2O
Votava, Brian L.	1LT	Medical-Surgical Nurse	66H00
Wade, John C.	LTC	Urologist	60k00
Wagner, Arliss F.	SGT	Practical Nurse, Medic	91C2O
Wahl, Jerome H.	CPT	Pharmacist	68H00
Wahlman, Daniel B.	SPC	Medical Specialist	91A1O
Wangler, Jocelyn J.	SPC	Medical Supply Specialist	76J1O
Wastjer, Roseann C.	SGT	Medical Specialist	91A2O
Watt, Mary E.	PFC	Hospital Food Service Sp'lst	91M1O
Weichel, Brian J.	SGT	Biomedical Equipment Sp'lst	35U3O
Weichel, Marlin G.	SPC	Medical Lab Specialist	92B2O

Weichel, Raymond D.	SPC	X-Ray Specialist	91P1O
Weichel Richard L.	SGT	Medical Lab Specialist	92B3O
Wells, Lyle J.	2LT	Medical-Surgical Nurse	66H00
Wentz, Jeanet C.	2LT	Medical-Surgical Nurse	66H00
Wenzel, Teresa M.	SPC	Medical Lab Specialist	92B1O
Werner, Davis J.	SPC	Radio Operator	31C1O
West, Kurtis A.	SPC	X-Ray Specialist	91P1O
Wetsch, Brenda L.	SPC	Administrative Specialist	71L1O
Wetsch, Jeffrey D.	SPC	ENT Specialist	91U1O
Wiggins, Deborah L.	SPC	Practical Nurse, Medic	91C2O
Williams, Latarsha D.	PV2	Medical Supply Specialist	76J1O
Wilson, Barry T.	SPC	Hospital Food Service Sp'lst	91M1O
Winchester, Mary A.	SSG	Biomedical Equipment Sp'lst	35U3O
Wishinskiy, Barbara E.	SSG	Practical Nurse, Medic	91C3O
Wolf, Leo A.	SGT	Hospital Food Service Sp'lst	91M2O
Wolff, Patricia K.	SPC	Medical Specialist	91A1O
Wood, William C.	CPT	Field Medical Assistant MSC	67B00
Zuspann, Charles W.	SPC	Personnel Administrative Ass't	75B1O

APPENDIX D
Organization for Typical Infantry: (For Armor see Paul Hook's interview in Chapter Six.)

A Squad is the smallest unit of the army—typically nine to ten soldiers—and usually a "noncom," meaning non-commissioned officer (NCO—i.e., a corporal or sergeant) is in charge. With highly trained specialists, there will likely be a more complicated organization.

A Platoon at full strength can contain sixteen to forty-four soldiers and two to four squads. The platoons are rarely at full strength and they are usually commanded by a lieutenant with an NCO as second in command.

A Company in today's army would be sixty-two to one hundred ninety soldiers.

A Battalion consists of three hundred to one thousand soldiers in four to six companies, and it is usually commanded by a Lt. Colonel or Colonel. When the 311th Army Reserve Hospital was recalled in 1990–1991 for Desert Storm, we were battalion-size with some twenty-four doctors and over four hundred personnel.

A Regiment is composed of two or more battalions—usually at least three.
A Brigade is composed of two to five battalions of three thousand to five thousand soldiers and it is usually commanded by—you guessed it!—a Brigadier General.

A Division is ten thousand to fifteen thousand soldiers in three or more brigades, and a two-star Major General commands it.

A Corp is thirty thousand to sixty thousand soldiers in two or more divisions, and a three-star Lieutenant General commands it.

APPENDIX E
Acronyms

- ACR   Armored Cavalry Regiment
- AFB   Air Force Base
- AMEDD   Army Medical Department
- AMEF   Army Medical Evacuation Facility
- ARCOM   Army Reserve Command
- ARTEP   Army Training Evaluation Program
- AWACS   Airborne Warning and Control System
- BDUs   Battle Dress Uniforms, Camouflaged, Fatigues.
- CALCUM   Conventional Air Launch Cruise Missile
- CONUS Continental United States
- DEPMEDS   Deployed Medical Equipment (in storage)
- EFL   Essential Force List
- EPW   Enemy Prisoner of War
- EVAC   Evacuation Hospital (20-24 doctors)
- FSCL   Fire Support Coordination Line
- GBU   Guided Bomb Unit
- LPN   Licensed Practical Nurse
- MASF   Mobile Air Staging Facility
- MASH   Mobile Army Surgical Hospital (6-8 doctors)
- MOB   Mobilization
- MOP   Massive Ordnance Penetrator
- MOPP   Mission Oriented Protective Posture
- MOPP (Gear)   Refers to the Chemical Suit, Boots, Gloves & Gas Mask
- MOS   Military Occupation Specialty

- MOSQ   Military Occupation Specialty Qualified
- MQS   Military Qualification Standards
- MUTA   Multiple Unit Training Assembly
- NAADS (Personnel)   New Army Authorization Documents System
- NCO   Non-commissioned Officer
- POM   Preparation for Overseas Movement
- POW   Prisoner of War
- RN   Registered Nurse RSNA   Radiological Society of North America
- SCUD   Western name for Soviet made missile series[157]
- SITREP Situation Report
- WOMAX (WWMCCS)   World Wide Military Command & Control System

---

157 Does not refer to any Soviet or Russian words, but is likely derived from the dictionary meaning of scud because the missile is designed to skim along under the clouds at low altitudes. The term actually originated from NATO (North Atlantic Treaty Organization) terminology.

APPENDIX F
Phonetic Alphabet

Alpha

Bravo

Charlie

Delta

Echo

Foxtrot

Golf

Hotel

India

Juliet

Kilo

Lima

Mike

November

Oscar

Papa

Quebec

Romeo

Sierra

Tango

Uniform

Victor

Whiskey

X-ray

Yankee

Zulu

APPENDIX G

Department of the Army
311ᵗʰ EVACUATION HOSPITAL
APO New York, NY 09686
Memorandum of Understanding
BETWEEN
MAFRAQ Hospital and 311ᵗʰ Evacuation Hospital

SUBJECT: Health care of military casualties in Mafraq Hospital

Peace be upon you,

This memorandum confirms an agreement reached on January 23, 1991. This agreement consists of the following items:

1. The two hospital staffs of doctor and nursing personnel will be fully integrated to provide comprehensive health care for any military or civilian patient during the time of this agreement.

2. Medical supplies, drugs and equipment provided by either hospital will be available to any patient admitted to this facility.

3. The following policies may be applied specifically to the United States and allied military and civilian patients:

    A. The Mafraq Hospital record will be used to document patient care. Any military forms may be added as appropriate. If the patient arrives with a military record already established, this record will be closed and the Mafraq record will be closed, and a military record will be opened. All Mafraq records will be photocopied to be placed, in the serviceman's military health record.

    B. The admitting doctor, either a Mafraq or 311ᵗʰ staff will be the primary doctor. In the case of civilian admissions, the admitting doctor will be Mafraq. In the case of a military patient, the admitting doctor will be 311th staff. Both staffs will be involved through consult. If a difference of medical opinion occurs and cannot be resolved, the primary physician will take responsibility so that appropriate records can be maintained. An on-call service will be available at all times. A Doctor's order sheet is recommended for Mafraq records and is a requirement for military patients.

C. 311th Evacuation Hospital Nursing Personnel will provide 24 hour nursing care for all military casualties. When possible specific wards will be designated to receive military casualties. These wards may be mixed male and female wards.

D. The 311th nursing staff will be encouraged to provide the level of patient care for which they are prepared. This includes starting IVs and blood and drawing blood for lab specimens, giving all types of drugs, changing dressings, accepting verbal orders from doctors, initiating CPR, and performing life or limb saving techniques.

4. The below signatures validate this agreement.

The below signatures validate this agreement.

Peace be upon you.

(signed)   (signed)

_____

Gerald Moyer   DR. Amin Al-Gohary

Colonel, MC   Deputy Director of Technical Affairs

Chief, Professional Services   Mafraq Hospital

311th Evacuation Hospital

____4 February, 1991_____   4 February, 1991

INDEX

ABOUT THE AUTHOR

William Franklin Hook, MD.

A graduate of Stanford University and the Jefferson Medical College of Jefferson University, Philadelphia, PA, Dr. Hook is a retired physician radiologist, an ex-Associate Clinical Professor of Radiology at the University of North Dakota's School of Medicine, and an author.

Dr. Hook's long and distinguished military career includes three years of active duty with the Navy including a year of sea duty, and service as a reserve Army officer. Colonel Hook commanded the 311th Evacuation Hospital during its deployment to the Middle East during the first Persian Gulf War (Desert Storm).

His military awards include the National Defense Medal with clusters, Armed Forces Reserve Medal, Army Service Ribbon, Army Reserve Component Medal, Overseas Service Ribbon, Armed Forces Expedition Medal, Meritorious Service Medal, Army Commendation Medal (Desert Storm), Liberation of Kuwait Medal (Saudi Government), and the Kuwait Liberation Medal.

Col. Hook belongs to the American Legion and is a lifetime member of the VFW. He currently lives in Hot Springs, South Dakota.

An additional selection of Dr. Hook's work can be seen on the University of North Dakota's Radiology web site.

He is an Associate Clinical Professor of Radiology (retired), University of North Dakota School of Medicine, a Diplomate of the American Board of Radiology and a Diplomate American Board of Nuclear Medicine.

Other Publications:
- *Never Subdued, A true narrative history of the Philippine-American War.* **CreateSpace, 2011.**
- *Common Sense and Modern First Aid.* **Published by the Bismarck Medical Foundation (1966).**

- *Complications of Cardiac Catheterization and Angiography* J Lancet. Vol. 88.6 (Jun 1968): 133-5.
- *Anterior Mediastinal Teratoids* Minnesota Medicine. Vol. 55.3 (Mar 1972): 238-9.
- *Pulmonary Embolism, Diagnosis & Management.* Reports of the Q & R Clinic. Vol. 4.3 (1984).
  - *Acute Tubular Necrosis*
    Ibid. Vol. 4.3 (1984).
  - *Four Phase Bone Scan*
    Ibid. Vol. 5.3 (1985).
  - *False Positive GI Bleed Scan*
    Ibid. Vol. 6.3 (1986).
  - *X-Ray Film Reading Made Easy*
    Text on CD ROM (2001).

See Dr. Hook's web sites at www.neversubdued.com and www.desertstormdiary.com

CPSIA information can be obtained
at www.ICGtesting.com
Printed in the USA
LVHW081553081119
636789LV00030B/773/P